THE BOOK OF
FIVE RINGS

THE BOOK OF
FIVE RINGS

MIYAMOTO MUSASHI

Translated by Victor Harris

SIRIUS

This edition published in 2024 by Sirius Publishing, a division of
Arcturus Publishing Limited,
26/27 Bickels Yard, 151–153 Bermondsey Street,
London SE1 3HA

ISBN: 978-1-3988-4076-8
AD011938UK

Printed in China

CONTENTS

INTRODUCTION

Japan during Musashi's lifetime

Miyamoto Musashi was born in 1584, in a Japan struggling to recover from more than four centuries of internal strife. The traditional rule of the emperors had been overthrown in the twelfth century, and although each successive emperor remained the figurehead of Japan, his powers were very much reduced. Since that time, Japan had seen almost continuous civil war between the provincial lords, warrior monks and brigands, all fighting one another for land and power. In the fifteenth and sixteenth centuries the lords, called *daimyō*, built huge stone castles to protect themselves and their lands, and castle towns outside the walls began to grow up.

In 1573, however, one man, Oda Nobunaga, came to the fore in Japan. He became the *shōgun*, or military dictator, and within nine years had succeeded in gaining control of almost the whole of the country. When Nobunaga was assassinated in 1582, a commoner took over the government. Toyotomi Hideyoshi continued the work of unifying Japan, ruthlessly putting down any traces of insurrection. He revived the old gulf between the warriors of Japan – the *samurai* – and the commoners by introducing restrictions on the wearing of swords. 'Hideyoshi's sword-hunt', as it was known, meant that only samurai were allowed to wear two swords; the short one which everyone could wear and the long one which distinguished the samurai from the rest of the population.

Although Hideyoshi did much to settle Japan and increase trade with the outside world, by the time of his death in 1598 internal disturbances still had not been completely eliminated. The real isolation and unification of Japan began with Tokugawa Ieyasu, a former associate of both Hideyoshi and Nobunaga, who formally became the *shōgun* of Japan after defeating Hideyoshi's son Hideyori at the Battle of Sekigahara in 1600. Ieyasu established his government at Edo, present-day Tokyo. His was a stable, peaceful government which began a period of Japanese history that lasted until the Imperial Restoration of 1868.

The traditional class consciousness of Japan hardened into a rigid class structure. There were basically four classes of person: samurai, farmers, artisans and merchants. The samurai were the highest and included the lords, senior government officials, warriors, and minor officials and foot soldiers. Next in the hierarchy came the farmers. Their lot was a rather unhappy one, as they were forced to give most of their crops to the lords and were not allowed to leave their farms. Then came the artisans and craftsmen, and last of all the merchants, who, though looked down upon, eventually rose to prominence because of the vast wealth they accumulated.

Musashi belonged to the samurai class. We find the origins of the samurai class in the *Kondei* ('stalwart youth') system established in AD 792, whereby the Japanese army was revived by stiffening the ranks with permanent training officers recruited from among the young sons of the high families. These officers were mounted, wore armour, and used the bow and sword.

When the great provincial armies were gradually disbanded under Hideyoshi and Ieyasu, many out-of-work samurai roamed the country redundant in an era of peace. Musashi was one such samurai, a *rōnin* or 'wave man'. The hordes of redundant samurai found themselves living in a society which was completely based on the old chivalry, but at the same time they were apart from a society in which there was no place for men at arms. Many *rōnin* put up their swords and became artisans, but others, like Musashi, pursued the ideal of the warrior searching for enlightenment through the perilous paths of Kendo. Duels of revenge and tests of skill were commonplace and fencing schools multiplied. This was the time of the flowering of the sword arts, or Kendo.

During Musashi's lifetime numerous schools sprang up in the new castle towns. Each *daimyō*, or lord, sponsored a Kendo school where his retainers could be trained and his sons educated. The hope of every *rōnin* was that he would defeat the students and master of a *dōjō* in combat, thus increasing his fame and bringing his name to the ears of one who might employ him.

The samurai wore two swords. The longer sword was carried out of doors only, while the shorter sword was worn at all times. For training, wooden or bamboo swords were often used. Duelling and other tests of arms were common, with both real and practice swords. These took place in fencing halls and before shrines, in the streets and within castle walls. Duels were fought to the death or until one of the contestants was disabled, but a few generations after Musashi's time the *shinai*, a pliable bamboo sword and, later, padded fencing armour came to be widely used. The samurai studied with all kinds of weapons, including halberds, sticks, swords and chain-and-sickle.

To train in Kendo one must subjugate the self, bear the pain of gruelling practice, and cultivate a level mind in the face of peril. But the Way of the sword means not only fencing training but also living by the code of honour of the samurai elite. Warfare was the spirit of the samurai's everyday life, and he could face death as if it were a domestic routine. The meaning of life and death by the sword was mirrored in the everyday conduct of the feudal Japanese, and he who realized the resolute acceptance of death at any moment in his everyday life was a master of the sword.

The life of Miyamoto Musashi

Shinmen Musashi no Kami Fujiwara no Genshin, better known as Miyamoto Musashi, was born in a village called Miyamoto in the province Mimasaka in 1584. Musashi's ancestors were a branch of the powerful Harima clan in Kyushu, the southern island of Japan. When Musashi was seven, his father, Munisai, either died or abandoned the child. As his mother had also died, Musashi was left in the care of an uncle on his mother's side, a priest. So we find Musashi an orphan during Hideyoshi's campaigns of unification, the son of a samurai in a violent, unhappy land.

He was a boisterous youth, strong-willed and physically large for his age. It is recorded that he slew a man in single combat when he was just thirteen years old. The opponent was Arima Kihei, a samurai of the *Shintō-ryū* school of military arts, skilled with sword and spear. Musashi's next contest was at the age of sixteen, when he defeated Tadashima Akiyama. About this time, he left home to embark on the 'Warrior Pilgrimage', which saw him victorious in scores of contests and took him to war six times.

In the Battle of Sekigahara, which resulted in Ieyasu succeeding Hideyoshi as shōgun of Japan, Musashi joined the ranks of the Ashikaga army to fight against Ieyasu. He endured the terrible three days during which seventy thousand people died, and he survived the hunting down and massacre of the vanquished army. He went up to Kyoto, the capital, when he was twenty-one. This was the scene of his vendetta against the Yoshioka family. The Yoshiokas had been fencing instructors to the Ashikaga house for generations. Munisai, Musashi's father, had been invited to Kyoto some years before by the shōgun, Ashikaga Yoshiaka. Munisai was a competent swordsman, and an expert with the *jitte*,

a kind of iron truncheon with a tongue for catching sword blades. The story has it that Munisai fought three of the Yoshiokas, winning two of the duels.

Musashi spent the following years wandering over Japan and becoming a legend in his own time. We find mention of his name and stories of his prowess in registers, diaries and on monuments, and in folk memory from Tokyo to Kyushu. He had more than sixty contests before he was twenty-nine, and won them all.

Musashi's most well-known duel was in the seventeenth year of Keicho, 1612, when he was in Ogura in Bunzen province. His opponent was Sasaki Kojiro, a young man who had developed a strong fencing technique known as *Tsubame-gaeshi* or 'swallow counter', inspired by the motion of a swallow's tail in flight. The place of the duel was to be an island some few miles from Ogura. That night, Musashi left his lodging and moved to the house of Kobayashi Tare Zaemon. This inspired a rumour that awe of Kojiro's subtle technique had made Musashi run away, afraid for his life.

As Sato rowed across to the island, Musashi fashioned a paper string to tie back the sleeves of his kimono, and cut a wooden sword from the spare oar. Kojiro and the waiting officials were astounded to see the strange figure of Musashi, with his unkempt hair tied up in a towel, leap from the boat brandishing the long wooden oar and rush through the

waves up the beach towards his enemy. Kojiro drew his long sword, a fine blade by Nagamitsu of Bizen, and threw away his scabbard. 'You have no more need of that,' said Musashi as he rushed forward with his sword held to one side. Kojiro was provoked into making the first cut and Musashi dashed upward at his blade, bringing the oar down on Kojiro's head. Musashi noted Kojiro's condition and bowed to the astounded officials before running back to his boat. Some sources have it that after he killed Kojiro, Musashi threw down the oar and, nimbly leaping back several paces, drew both his swords and flourished them with a shout at his fallen enemy.

Musashi finally settled down at the age of fifty, and spent his time living apart from society while he devoted himself with a ferocious single-mindedness to the search for enlightenment by the Way of the sword.

He is known to the Japanese as Kensei, that is, 'sword saint'. *The Book of Five Rings* is unique among books on martial art and heads every Kendo bibliography. It deals with the strategy of warfare and the methods of single combat in exactly the same way. It is, in Musashi's words, 'a guide for men who want to learn strategy', and is Musashi's last will, the key to the path he trod. When, at twenty-eight or twenty-nine, he had become such a strong fighter, he did not settle down and build a school, replete with success, but became doubly engrossed with his study. In his last days even, he scorned the life of comfort with Lord Hosokawa and lived two years alone in a mountain cave, deep in contemplation.

Musashi wrote, 'When you have attained the Way of strategy there will be not one thing that you cannot understand' and 'You will see the Way in everything.' He also produced masterpieces of ink painting, works in metal, and founded a school of sword-guard makers.

He wrote 'Study the Ways of all professions' and it is evident that he did just this. He sought out not only great swordsmen but also priests, strategists, artists and craftsmen, eager to broaden his knowledge.

Musashi writes about the various aspects of Kendo in such a way that it is possible for the beginner to study at beginner's level and for Kendo masters to study the same words on a higher level. This applies not just to military strategy, but to any situation where plans and tactics are used. Japanese businessmen have used *The Book of Five Rings* as a guide for business practice, turning sales campaigns into military operations by employing the same energetic methods.

Victor Harris

五輪書

THE BOOK OF FIVE RINGS

兵法の道、二天一流と号し、
数年鍛練の事、始て書物に顕さんと思、
時、寛永二十年十月上旬の比、
九州肥後の地岩戸山に上り、
天を拝し、觀音を礼し、佛前に向。
生國播磨の武士、新免武藏守藤原玄信、
年つもりて六十。
われ若年の昔より、兵法の道に心をかけ、
十三歳にして始て勝負をす。
其あひて、新當流有馬喜兵衛と云兵法者
にうち勝、十六歳にして、
但馬國秋山と云強力の兵法者に打かち、
二十一歳にして、都へのぼり、
天下の兵法者に逢、数度の勝負をけつすと
いへども、勝利を得ざると云事なし。

I have been many years training in the Way[1] of strategy, called *Niten Ichi Ryu*, and now I think I will explain it in writing for the first time.

It is now during the first ten days of the tenth month in the twentieth year of Kanei (1645). I have climbed mountain Iwato of Higo in Kyushu to pay homage to heaven[2], pray to Kwannon[3], and kneel before Buddha. I am a warrior of Harima province, Shinmen Musashi no Kami Fujiwara no Genshin, age sixty years.

From youth, my heart has been inclined toward the Way of strategy. My first duel was when I was thirteen; I struck down a strategist of the Shinto school, one Arima Kihei. When I was sixteen, I struck down an able strategist, Tadashima Akiyama. When I was twenty-one, I went up to the capital and met all manner of strategists, never once failing to win in many contests.

其後、國々所々に至り、諸流の兵法者に行合、
六十餘度迄勝負をすといへども、
一度も其利をうしなはず。
其程、年十三より二十八九迄の事也。
われ三十を越て、跡をおもひミるに、
兵法至極してかつにハあらず。
をのづから道の器用ありて、天理をはなれざる故か、
又ハ、他流の兵法不足なる所にや。
其後、猶も深き道理を得んと、
朝鍛夕錬して見れバ、をのづから
兵法の道に逢事、我五十歳の比也。
それより以來は、
尋入べき道なくして光陰を送る。
兵法の利に任て、諸藝諸能の道となせバ、
万事におゐて、われに師匠なし。
今此書を作るといへども、
佛法儒道の古語をもからず、
軍記軍法のふるき事をも用ひず。
此一流のミたて、實の心を顯す事、
天道と觀世音を鏡として、
十月十日の夜、寅の一天に
筆をとつて、書始るもの也。

After that I went from province to province, duelling with strategists of various schools, and not once failed to win even though I had as many as sixty encounters. This was between the ages of thirteen and twenty-eight or twenty-nine. When I reached thirty, I looked back on my past. The previous victories were not due to my having mastered strategy. Perhaps it was natural ability, or the order of heaven, or that other schools' strategy was inferior.

After that, I studied morning and evening, searching for the principle, and came to realize the Way of strategy when I was fifty. Since then I have lived without following any particular Way. Thus, with the virtue of strategy, I practise many arts and abilities – all things with no teacher. To write this book I did not use the law of Buddha or the teachings of Confucius, neither old war chronicles nor books on martial tactics. I take up my brush to explain the true spirit of this Ichi school as it is mirrored in the Way of heaven and Kwannon.

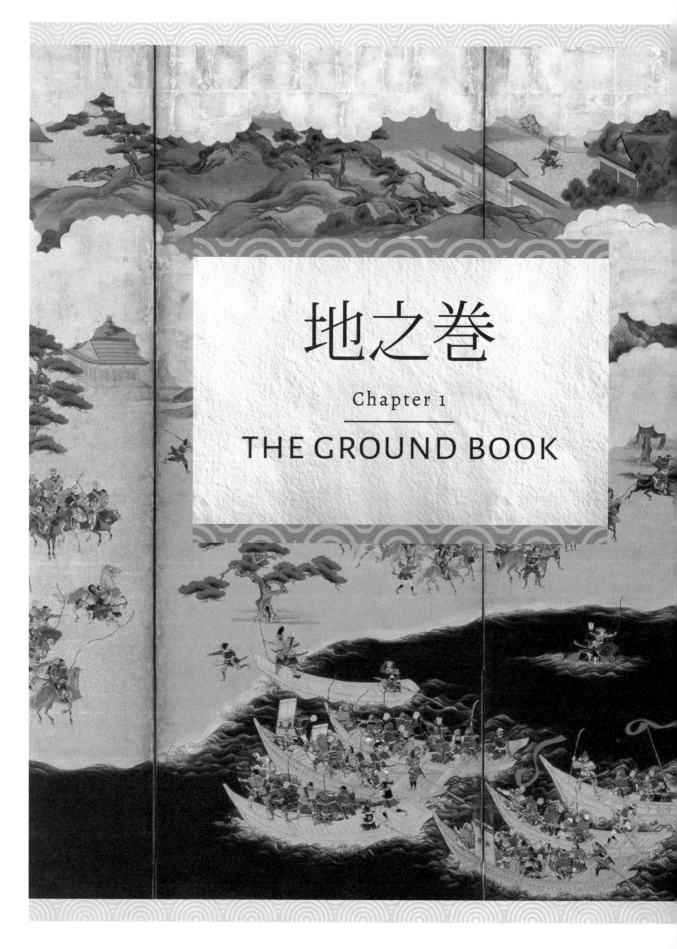

地之巻

Chapter 1

THE GROUND BOOK

夫、兵法と云事、武家の法也。
将たるものハ、とりわき此法をおこなひ、
卒たる者も、此道を知べき事なり。
今世の間に、兵法の道、たしかに
わきまへたると云武士なし。
先、道を顕して有ハ、佛法として
人をたすくる道、又、儒道として文の道を糺し、
醫者と云て諸病を治する道、
或は歌道者とて和歌の道をおしへ、
或ハ数寄者、弓法者、其外、諸藝諸能までも、
思ひ／＼に稽古し、心々にすくもの也。
兵法の道にハ、すく人まれなり。
先、武士ハ、文武二道と云て、
二の道を嗜む事、是道也。

Strategy is the craft of the warrior. Commanders must enact the craft, and troopers should know this Way. There is no warrior in the world today who really understands the Way of strategy. There are various Ways. There is the Way of salvation by the law of Buddha, the Way of Confucius governing the Way of learning, the Way of healing as a doctor, as a poet teaching the Way of Waka,[5] tea, archery,[6] and many arts and skills. Each man practises as he feels inclined. It is said that the warrior's is the twofold Way of pen and sword,[7] and he should have a taste for both Ways.

たとひ此道不器用なりとも、
武士たるものハ、おのれ／＼が分才ほどは、
兵の法をバ勤むべき事也。
大かた武士の思ふ心をはかるに、
武士ハたゞ、死（る）と云道を嗜む事と
覚ゆるほどの儀也。
死（る）道におゐてハ、武士ばかりに限らず、
出家にても女にても、百姓以下に至迄、
義理をしり、恥をおもひ、死する所を
思ひきる事は、其差別なきもの也。
武士の兵法をおこなふ道ハ、
何事におゐても、人にすぐるゝ所を本とし、
或ハ一身の切合に勝、或ハ数人の戦に勝、
主君のため我身のため、
名をあげ身をもたてんとおもふ、
これ兵法の徳を以てなり。

Even if a man has no natural ability, he can be a warrior by sticking assiduously to both divisions of the Way. Generally speaking, the Way of the warrior is resolute acceptance of death.[8] Although not only warriors but priests, women, peasants and lowlier folk have been known to die readily in the cause of duty or out of shame, this is a different thing. The warrior is different in that studying the Way of strategy is based on overcoming men. Through victory gained in crossing swords with individuals, or enjoining battle with large numbers, we can attain power and fame for ourselves or for our lord. This is the virtue of strategy.

兵法の道

漢土和朝迄も、此道をおこなふものを、
兵法達者と云傳たり。
武士として、此法を学ばずと云事有べからず。
近代、兵法者と云て世をわたるもの、
これハ劔術一通りの儀也。
常陸國鹿嶋かんとりの社人共、
明神の傳として流々を立て、
國々を廻り人に傳事、近き比の事也。
いにしへより十能七藝とあるうちに、
利方と云て、藝にわたるといへ共、
利方と云出すより、
劔術一通りにかぎるべからず。
劔術一へんの利までにてハ、劔術もしりがたし。

The Way of strategy

In China and Japan, practitioners of the Way have been known as 'masters of strategy'.
Warriors must learn this Way.

Recently there have been people getting on in the world as strategists, but they are usually just sword-fencers. The attendants of the Kashima Kantori shrines[9] of the province Hitachi received instruction from the gods, and made schools based on this teaching, travelling from country to country instructing men. This is the recent meaning of strategy.

In olden times, strategy was listed among the Ten Abilities and Seven Arts as a beneficial practice. It was certainly an art, but as beneficial practice it was not limited to sword-fencing. The true value of sword-fencing cannot be seen within the confines of sword-fencing technique.

世の中を見るに、諸藝をうり物に仕立、
わが身をうり物の様に思ひ、
諸道具に付ても、うり物にこしらゆる心、
花實の二つにして、
花よりも実のすくなき所也。
とりわき此兵法の道に、
色をかざり花をさかせて、術をてらし、
或ハ一道場、二道場など云て、此道をおしへ、
此道を習て利を得んと思事、
誰か謂、なまへいほう大きずのもと、
誠なるべし。

If we look at the world, we see arts for sale. Men use equipment to sell their own selves. As if with the nut and the flower, the nut has become less than the flower. In this kind of Way of strategy, both those teaching and those learning the way are concerned with colouring and showing off their technique, trying to hasten the bloom of the flower. They speak of 'This Dōjō' and 'That Dōjō'. They are looking for profit. Someone once said, 'Immature strategy is the cause of grief'. That was a true saying.

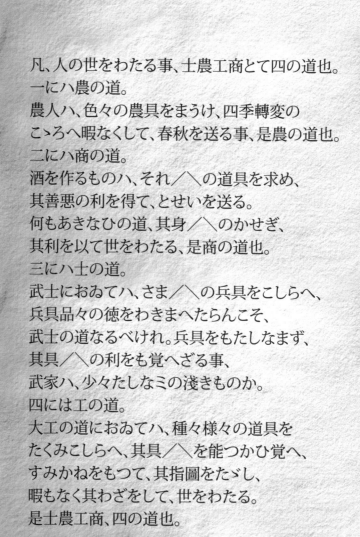

凡、人の世をわたる事、士農工商とて四の道也。
一にハ農の道。
農人ハ、色々の農具をまうけ、四季轉変の
こゝろへ暇なくして、春秋を送る事、是農の道也。
二にハ商の道。
酒を作るものハ、それ／＼の道具を求め、
其善悪の利を得て、とせいを送る。
何もあきなひの道、其身／＼のかせぎ、
其利を以て世をわたる、是商の道也。
三にハ士の道。
武士におゐてハ、さま／＼の兵具をこしらへ、
兵具品々の徳をわきまへたらんこそ、
武士の道なるべけれ。兵具をもたしなまず、
其具／＼の利をも覚へざる事、
武家ハ、少々たしなミの淺きものか。
四には工の道。
大工の道におゐてハ、種々様々の道具を
たくみこしらへ、其具／＼を能つかひ覚へ、
すみかねをもつて、其指圖をたゞし、
暇もなく其わざをして、世をわたる。
是士農工商、四の道也。

The Four Ways

There are four Ways in which men pass through life: as gentlemen, farmers, artisans and merchants.

The Way of the farmer: using agricultural instruments, he sees springs through to autumns with an eye on the changes of season.

Second is the Way of the merchant. The winemaker obtains his ingredients and puts them to use to make his living. The Way of the merchant is always to live by taking profit. This is the Way of the merchant.

Thirdly the gentleman warrior, carrying the weaponry of his Way. The Way of the warrior is to master the virtue of his weapons. If a gentleman dislikes strategy he will not appreciate the benefit of weaponry, so must he not have a little taste for this?

Fourthly the Way of the artisan. The Way of the carpenter[10] is to become proficient in the use of his tools, first to lay his plans with a true measure and then perform his work according to plan. Thus, he passes through life.

These are the Four Ways – of the gentleman, the farmer, the artisan and the merchant.

兵法の道を大工にたとえる事

兵法を、大工の道にたとへて云顕す也。
大工にたとゆる事、家と云事に付ての儀也。
公家、武家、四家、
其家の破れ、家のつゞくと云事、
其流、其風、其家などゝいへバ、
家と云より、大工の道にたとへたり。
大工は、大にたくむと書くなれバ、
兵法の道、大なるたくミによつて、
大工に云なぞらへて書顕す也。
兵の法を学ばんと思はゞ、此書を思案して、
師は針、弟子は糸となつて、
たへず稽古有べき事也。
大将ハ、大工の棟梁として、
天下のかねをわきまへ、其国のかねを糺し、
其家のかねをしる事、棟梁の道也。
大工の棟梁ハ、堂塔伽藍のすみかねを覚へ、
くうでんろうかくの指圖をしり、
人々をつかひ、家々を取立事、
大工の棟梁、武家の棟梁も同じ事也。

Comparing the Way of the carpenter to strategy

The comparison with carpentry is through the connection with houses. Houses of the nobility, houses of warriors, the Four Houses,[11] ruin of houses, thriving of houses, the style of the house, the tradition of the house, and the name of the house. The carpenter uses a master plan of the building, and the Way of strategy is similar in that there is a plan of campaign. If you want to learn the craft of war, ponder over this book. The teacher is as a needle, the disciple is as thread. You must practise constantly.

Like the foreman carpenter, the commander must know natural rules, and the rules of the country, and the rules of houses. This is the Way of the foreman.

The foreman carpenter must know the architectural theory of towers and temples, and the plans of palaces, and must employ men to raise up houses. The Way of the foreman carpenter is the same as the Way of the commander of a warrior house.

家を立るに、木くばりする事、
直にして節もなく、見付のよきを表の柱とし、
少ふしありとも直に強きを裏の柱とし、
たとひ少弱くとも、節なき木のミさまよきをバ、
敷居、鴨居、戸障子と、それ／＼につかひ、
節有とも、ゆがみたりとも、強き木をバ、
其家のつよみ／＼を見分て、能吟味して
つかふにおゐてハ。
又、材木のうちにしても、
節おほく、ゆがミてよハきをバ、あしゝろともなし、
後には薪ともなすべき事也。
棟梁におゐて、大工をつかふ事、
其上中下を知り、或ハ床まはり、
或ハ戸障子、或ハ敷居、鴨居、
天井巳下、それ／＼につかひて、
あしきにハ、ねだをはらせ、
猶悪きにハ、くさびを削せ、
人を見分てつかへバ、
其渉行て、手ぎハ能もの也。
はかのゆき、手ぎハよきと云所、
物ごとをゆるさゞる事、たいゆうを知る事、
氣の上中下を知事、いさみをつくると云事、
むたいを知と云事、
か様の事ども、棟梁の心持に有事也。
兵法の利、かくのごとし。

In the construction of houses, choice of woods is made. Straight unknotted timber of good appearance is used for the revealed pillars, straight timber with small defects is used for the inner pillars. Timber of the finest appearance, even if a little weak, is used for the thresholds, lintels, doors, and sliding doors,[12] and so on. Good, strong timber, though it be gnarled and knotted, can always be used discreetly in construction. Timber which is weak or knotted throughout should be used as scaffolding, and later for firewood.

The foreman carpenter allots his men work according to their ability. Floor layers, makers of sliding doors, thresholds and lintels, ceilings and so on. Those of lesser ability lay the floor joists, carve wedges and do such miscellaneous work. If the foreman knows and deploys his men well, the finished work will be good. The foreman should take into account the abilities and limitations of his men, circulating among them and asking nothing unreasonable. He should know their morale and spirit, and encourage them when necessary. This is the same as the principle of strategy.

兵法の道

士卒たるものハ大工にして、
手づから其道具をとぎ、
色々のせめ道具をこしらへ、
大工の箱に入てもち、
棟梁の云付る所をうけ、
柱、かうりやうをも、てうなにてけづり、
床棚をもかんなにて削り、
すかし物、彫物をもして、
能かねを糺し、すミ／＼めんだうまでも、
手ぎハよく仕立所、大工の法也。
大工のわざ、手にかけてよく仕覚へ、
すミかねをよくしれば、後は棟梁となるもの也。
大工の嗜、能きるゝ道具をもち、
すき／＼にとぐ事肝要也。
其道具をとつて、御厨子、書棚、机つくゑ、
又は行燈、まな板、なべのふた迄も、
達者にする所、大工の専也。
士卒たる者、此ごとくなり。能々吟味有べし。
大工の嗜、ひづまざる事、とめを合する事、
かんなにて能削事、すり（ミ）かゝざる事、
後にひすかざる事、肝要也。
此道を学ばんと思はゞ、
書顕す所の一こと／＼に心を入て、
よく吟味有べき者也。

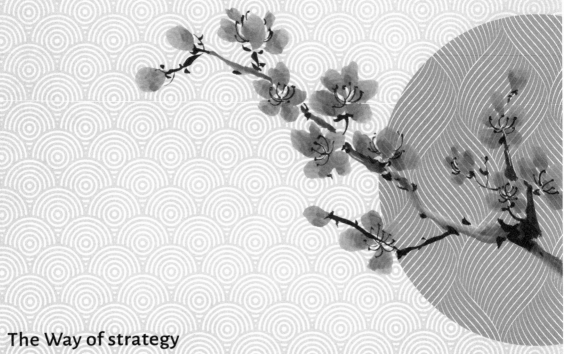

The Way of strategy

Like a trooper, the carpenter sharpens his own tools. He carries his equipment in his tool box, and works under the direction of his foreman. He makes columns and girders with an axe, shapes floorboards and shelves with a plane, cuts fine openwork and carvings accurately, giving as excellent a finish as his skill will allow. This is the craft of the carpenters. When the carpenter grows to be skilled and understands measures, he can become a foreman.

The carpenter's attainment is, having tools which will cut well, to make small shrines,[13] writing shelves, tables, paper lanterns, chopping boards and pot-lids. These are the specialities of the carpenter. Things are similar for the trooper. You ought to think deeply about this.

The attainment of the carpenter is that his work is not warped, that the joints are not misaligned, and that the work is truly planed so that it meets well and is not merely finished in sections. This is essential. If you want to learn this Way, deeply consider the things written in this book one at a time. You must do sufficient research.

此兵法の書、五巻に仕立事。

五ツの道をわかち、一巻／＼にして、
其利をしらしめんために、
地水火風空として、五巻に書顕すなり。
地之巻におゐてハ、
兵法の道の大躰、我一流の見立、
劍術一通りにしてハ、まことの道を得がたし。
大なる所より、ちいさきところをしり、
淺より深きに至る。
直なる道の地形を引ならすに依て、
初を地之巻と名付る也。
第二、水之巻。
水を本として、心を水になす也。
水ハ、方圓の器にしたがひ、
一てきとなり、さうかいとなる。
水にへきたんの色あり。清き所をもちゐて、
一流の事を此巻に書顕也。
劍術一通の理、さだかに見分、
一人の敵に自由に勝ときハ、
世界の人に皆勝所也。
人に勝といふ心ハ、千万の敵にも同意なり。
将たるものゝ兵法、ちいさきを大になす事、
尺のかねを以て大佛をたつるに同じ。
か様の儀、こまやかには書分がたし。
一を以万を知る事、兵法の利也。
一流の事、此水の巻に書記すなり。

Outline of the five books of this book of strategy

The Way is shown in five books[14] concerning different aspects. These are Ground, Water, Fire, Tradition (Wind), and Void.[15]

The body of the Way of strategy from the viewpoint of my Ichi school is explained in the Ground Book. It is difficult to realize the true Way just through sword-fencing. Know the smallest things and the biggest things, the shallowest things and the deepest things. As if it were a straight road mapped out on the ground, the first book is called the Ground Book.

Second is the Water Book. With water as the basis, the spirit becomes like water. Water adopts the shape of its receptacle, it is sometimes a trickle and sometimes a wild sea. Water has a clear blue colour. By the clarity, things of Ichi school are shown in this book. If you master the principles of sword-fencing, when you freely beat one man, you beat any man in the world. The spirit of defeating a man is the same for ten million men. The strategist makes small things into big things, like building a great Buddha from a one-foot model. I cannot write in detail how this is done. The principle of strategy is having one thing, to know ten thousand things. Things of the Ichi school are written in this, the Water Book.

第三、火之巻。
此巻に戦の事を書記す也。
火ハ大小となり、けやけき心なるによつて、
合戦の事を書也。
合戦の道、一人と一人との戦も、
萬と萬との戦も同じ道也。
心を大なる事になし、心をちいさくなして、
よく吟味して見るべし。
大なる所は見へやすし、
ちいさき所は見へがたし。其子細、
大人数の事ハ、そくざにもとをりがたし。
一人の事ハ、心ひとつにてかはる事はやき
に依て、ちいさき所しる事得がたし。
能吟味有べし。
此火の巻の事、はやき間の事なるに依て、
日々に手なれ、常の事とおもひ、
心の替らぬ所、兵法の肝要也。然に依て、
戦勝負の所を、火之巻に書顕す也。

Third is the Fire Book. This book is about fighting. The spirit of fire is fierce, whether the fire be small or big; and so it is with battles. The Way of battles is the same for man to man fights and for 10,000 a side battles. You must appreciate that spirit can become big or small. What is big is easy to perceive: what is small is difficult to perceive. In short, it is difficult for large numbers of men to change position, so their movements can be easily predicted. An individual can easily change his mind, so his movements are difficult to predict. You must appreciate this. The essence of this book is that you must train day and night in order to make quick decisions. In strategy, it is necessary to treat training as a part of normal life with your spirit unchanging. Thus, combat in battle is described in the Fire Book.

第四、風之巻。

此巻を風之巻と記す事、我一流の事に非ず。

世の中の兵法、其流々の事を書のする所也。

風と云におゐてハ、昔の風、今の風、

其家々の風などゝあれバ、世間の兵法、

其流々のしわざを、さだかに書顕す、是風也。

他の事をよくしらずしてハ、

ミずからのわきまへなりがたし。

道々事々をおこなふに、外道と云心有。

日々に其道を勤と云とも、心の背けば、

其身ハ能道とおもふとも、直なる所よりみれば、

実の道にハあらず。

実の道を極めざれバ、少心のゆがみにつゐて、

後にハ大にゆがむもの也。

よく吟味すべし。

他の兵法、劔術ばかり、と世におもふ事、尤也。

わが兵法の利わざにおゐてハ、各別の儀也。

世間の兵法をしらしめんために、

風之巻として、他流の事を書顕す也。

Fourthly the Wind Book. This book is not concerned with my Ichi school, but with other schools of strategy. By Wind, I mean old traditions, present-day traditions, and family traditions of strategy. Thus I clearly explain the strategies of the world. This is tradition. It is difficult to know yourself if you do not know others. To all Ways there are side tracks. If you study a Way daily, and your spirit diverges, you may think you are obeying a good way, but objectively it is not the true Way. If you are following the true Way and diverge a little, this will later become a large divergence. You must realize this. Other strategies have come to be thought of as mere sword-fencing, and it is not unreasonable that this should be so. The benefit of my strategy, although it includes sword-fencing, lies in a separate principle. I have explained what is commonly meant by strategy in other schools in the Tradition (Wind) Book (see page 176).

豊芥峑塩島

第五、空之巻。
此巻、空と書顕す事。
空と云出すよりしてハ、
何をか奥と云、何をかくちといはん。
道理を得てハ道理を離れ、
兵法の道におのれと自由有て、
おのれと奇特を得、
時にあひてハ拍子をしり、
おのづから打、おのづからあたる、
是皆空の道也。
おのれと實の道に入事を、
空の巻にして書とゞむるもの也。

Fifthly, the Book of the Void. By Void, I mean that which has no beginning and no end. Attaining this principle means not attaining the principle. The Way of strategy is the Way of nature. When you appreciate the power of nature, knowing the rhythm of any situation, you will be able to hit the enemy naturally and strike naturally. All this is the Way of the Void. I intend to show how to follow the true Way according to nature in the Book of the Void.

二刀一流という名

二刀と云出す所、武士ハ、
将卒ともに、直に二刀を腰に付る役也。
昔ハ、太刀、刀と云、今ハ、刀、脇指と云。
武士たる者の此両腰を持事、
こまかに書顕すに及ばず。
我朝におゐて、しるもしらぬも、
こしにおぶ事、武士の道也。
此二ツの利をしらしめんために、
二刀一流と云也。

鑓長刀よりしてハ、外の物と云て、
武道具の内也。
一流の道、初心の者におゐて、
太刀、刀両手に持て、道を仕習ふ事、実の所也。
一命を捨るときハ、道具を殘さず役に立度もの也。
道具を役にたてず、腰に納て死する事、
本意にあるべからず。

Niten Ichi Ryu Ni To (one school – two swords)

Warriors, both commanders and troopers, carry two swords[16] at their belt. In olden times these were called the long sword and the sword; nowadays they are known as the sword and the companion sword. Let it suffice to say that in our land, whatever the reason, a warrior carries two swords at his belt. It is the Way of the warrior. Niten Ichi Ryu shows the advantage of using both swords.

The spear and halberd[17] are weapons which are carried out of doors. Students of the Ichi school Way of strategy should train from the start with the sword and long sword in either hand. This is the truth: when you sacrifice your life, you must make fullest use of your weaponry. It is false not to do so, and to die with a weapon yet undrawn.

然ども、両手に物を持事、
左右ともに自由にハ叶がたし。
太刀を片手にて取習ハせんため也。
鑓長刀、大道具ハ是非に及ばず、
刀脇差におゐてハ、
何れも片手にて持道具也。
太刀を両手にて持て悪しき事、
馬上にて悪し、かけはしる時、あしゝ、
沼ふけ、石原、さかしき道、人こミに悪し。
左に弓鑓を持、其外何れの道具を持ても、
皆片手にて太刀をつかふ物なれば、
両手にて太刀を構る事、実の道にあらず。
若、片手にて打ころしがたきときハ、
両手にても打とむべし。
手間の入事にても有べからず
先、片手にて太刀を振ならわせんために、
二刀として、太刀を片手にて振覚る道也。
人毎に始て取付時ハ、
太刀重くて振廻しがたき物なれども、
萬、始てとり付ときハ、
弓もひきがたし、長刀も振がたし。
何れも其道具／＼に馴てハ、弓も力強くなり、
太刀も振つけぬれバ、
道の力を得て振よくなる也。
太刀の道と云事、はやく振にあらず。
第二、水の巻にて知べし。
太刀ハ廣き所にて振、
脇指ハせばき所にてふる事、

先、道の本意也。
此一流におゐて、長きにても勝、
短にても勝故によつて、太刀の寸を定めず。
何れにても勝事を得るこゝろ、一流の道也。
太刀ひとつ持たるよりも、二つ持て能所、
大勢を一人して戦時、
又とり籠りものなどのときに、能事あり。
か様の儀、今委しく書顕すにおよばず。
一を以て万をしるべし。
兵法の道、おこなひ得てハ、
ひとつも見へずと云事なし。
能々吟味有べき也。

If you hold a sword with both hands, it is difficult to wield it freely to left and right, so my method is to carry the sword in one hand. This does not apply to large weapons such as the spear or halberd, but swords and companion swords can be carried in one hand. It is encumbering to hold a sword in both hands when you are on horseback, when running on uneven roads, on swampy ground, muddy rice fields, stony ground, or in a crowd of people. To hold the long sword in both hands is not the true Way, for if you carry a bow or spear or other arms in your left hand you have only one hand free for the long sword. However, when it is difficult to cut an enemy down with one hand, you must use both hands. It is not difficult to wield a sword in one hand; the Way to learn this is to train with two long swords, one in each hand. It will seem difficult at first, but everything is difficult at first. Bows are difficult to draw, halberds are difficult to wield; as you become accustomed to the bow so your pull will become stronger. When you become used to wielding the long sword, you will gain the power of the Way and wield the sword well.

As I will explain in the second book, the Water Book, there is no fast way of wielding the long sword. The long sword should be wielded broadly, and the companion sword closely. This is the first thing to realize.

According to this Ichi school, you can win with a long weapon, and yet you can also win with a short weapon. In short, the Way of the Ichi school is the spirit of winning, whatever the weapon and whatever its size.

It is better to use two swords rather than one when you are fighting a crowd, and especially if you want to take a prisoner.

These things cannot be explained in detail. From one thing, know ten thousand things. When you attain the Way of strategy there will not be one thing you cannot see. You must study hard.

太刀の徳

此道におゐて、太刀を振得たるものを、
兵法者と世に云傳たり。武藝の道に至て、
弓を能射れば、射手と云、
鉄炮を得たる者ハ、鉄炮打と云、
鑓をつかひ得てハ、鑓つかひと云、
長刀を覚てハ、長刀つかひと云。
然におゐてハ、太刀の道を覚へたるものを、
太刀つかひ、脇指つかひといはん事也。
弓鉄炮、鑓長刀、皆是武家の道具なれば、
何も兵法の道也。然ども、
太刀よりして、兵法と云事、道理也。
太刀の徳よりして、
世を治、身をおさむる事なれば、
太刀ハ兵法のおこる所也。
太刀の徳を得てハ、一人して十人に必勝事也。
一人して十人に勝なれば、
百人して千人に勝、千人して万人に勝。
然によつて、我一流の兵法に、
一人も万人もおなじ事にして、
武士の法を残らず、兵法と云所也。
道におゐて、儒者、佛者、
数奇者、しつけ者、乱舞者、
これらの事ハ、武士の道にてハなし。
其道にあらざるといへども、
道を廣くしれば、物ごとに出合事也。
いづれも、人間におゐて、
我道々を能ミがく事、肝要也。

The virtue of the long sword

Masters of the long sword are called strategists. As for the other military arts, those who master the bow are called archers, those who master the spear are called spearmen, those who master the gun[18] are called marksmen, those who master the halberd are called halberdiers. But we do not call masters of the Way of the long sword 'long-swordsmen', nor do we speak of 'companion-swordsmen'. Because bows, guns, spears and halberds are all warriors' equipment, they are certainly part of strategy. To master the virtue of the long sword is to govern the world and oneself, thus the long sword is the basis of strategy. The principle is 'strategy by means of the long sword'. If he attains the virtue of the long sword, one man can beat ten men. Just as one man can beat ten, so a hundred men can beat a thousand, and a thousand men can beat ten thousand. In my strategy, one man is the same as ten thousand, so this strategy is the complete warrior's craft.

The Way of the warrior does not include other Ways, such as Confucianism, Buddhism, certain traditions, artistic accomplishments and dancing.[19] But even though these are not part of the Way, if you know the Way broadly you will see it in everything. Men must polish their particular Way.

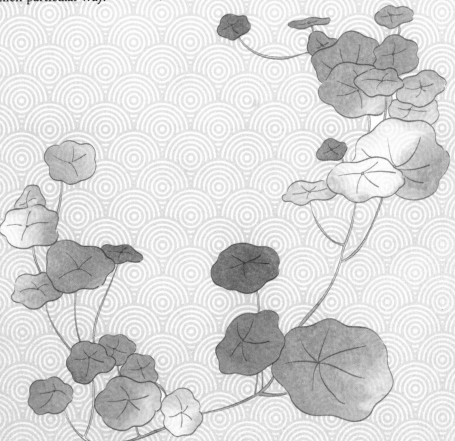

兵法に武具の利を知と云事

武具の利をわきまゆるに、何れの道具にても、
おりにふれ、時にしたがひ、出合もの也。
脇指は、座のせばき所、
敵のミぎハへよりて、其利多し。
太刀ハ、何れの所にても、大かた出合利有。
長刀ハ、戦場にてハ鑓におとる心あり。
鑓ハ先手也、長刀ハ後手也。
おなじ位のまなびにしてハ、鑓は少強し。
鑓長刀も、事により、
つまりたる所にてハ、其利すくなし。
とり籠りものなどに然るべからず。
只戦場の道具なるべし。
合戦の場にしてハ、肝要の道具也。
されども、座敷にての利を覚へ、
こまやかに思ひ、実の道を忘る>におゐてハ、
出合がたかるべし。

The benefit of weapons in strategy

There is a time and a place for use of weapons.

The best use of the companion sword is in a confined space, or when you are engaged closely with an opponent. The long sword can be used effectively in all situations.

The halberd is inferior to the spear on the battlefield. With the spear, you can take the initiative; the halberd is defensive. In the hands of one of two men of equal ability, the spear gives a little extra strength. Spear and halberd both have their uses, but neither is very beneficial in confined spaces. They cannot be used for taking a prisoner. They are essentially weapons for the field.

Anyway, if you learn 'indoor' techniques,[20] you will think narrowly and forget the true Way. Thus, you will have difficulty in actual encounters.

弓ハ、合戦の場にて、かけひきにも出合、
鑓わき、其外ものきハ／＼にて、
早く取合する物なれば、
野相の合戦などに、とりわき能物也。
城責など、又敵相二十間を越てハ、
不足なるもの也。
當世におゐてハ、弓は申に及ばず、
諸藝花多して、実すくなし。
左様の藝能は、肝要の時、役に立難し。
城郭の内にしてハ、鉄炮にしく事なし。
野相などにても、
合戦のはじまらぬうちにハ、其利多し。
戦はじまりてハ、不足なるべし。
弓の一徳は、はなつ矢、
人の目に見へてよし。
鉄炮の玉ハ、目にみへざる所不足なり。
此儀、能々吟味あるべき事（也）。
馬の事、強くこたへて、くせなき事、肝要也。
惣而、武道具につけ、馬も大かたにありき、
刀脇差も大かたにきれ、鑓長刀も大方にとをり、
弓鉄炮もつよくそこねざる様に有べし。
道具以下にも、かたわけてすく事あるべからず。
あまりたる事ハ、たらぬとおなじ事也。
人まねをせずとも、我身にしたがひ、
武道具は、手にあふやうに有べし。
将卒ともに、物にすき、物を嫌ふ事、悪し。
工夫肝要也。

The bow is tactically strong at the commencement of battle, especially battles on a moor, as it is possible to shoot quickly from among the spearmen. However, it is unsatisfactory in sieges, or when the enemy is more than forty yards away. For this reason there are now few traditional schools of archery. There is little use today for this kind of skill.

From inside fortifications, the gun has no equal among weapons. It is the supreme weapon on the field before the ranks clash, but once swords are crossed the gun becomes useless. One of the virtues of the bow is that you can see the arrows in flight and correct your aim accordingly, whereas gunshot cannot be seen. You must appreciate the importance of this.

Just as a horse must have endurance and no defects, so it is with weapons. Horses should walk strongly, and swords and companion swords should cut strongly. Spears and halberds must stand up to heavy use: bows and guns must be sturdy. Weapons should be hardy rather than decorative.

You should not have a favourite weapon. To become over-familiar with one weapon is as much a fault as not knowing it sufficiently well. You should not copy others, but use weapons which you can handle properly. It is bad for commanders and troopers to have likes and dislikes. These are things you must learn thoroughly.

兵法の拍子の事

物ごとにつき、拍子ハ有ものなれども、
取わき兵法の拍子、
鍛練なくしてハ、及がたき所也。
世の中の拍子、顕て有事、
乱舞の道、伶人管弦の拍子など、
是皆よくあふ所のろくなる拍子也。
武藝の道にわたつて、弓を射、鉄炮を放し、
馬に乗事迄も、拍子調子ハ有、
諸藝諸能に至ても、拍子を背事ハ有べからず。
又、空なる事におゐても、拍子ハあり、
武士の身の上にして、
奉公に身をしあぐる拍子、しさぐる拍子、
はずの相拍子、はずのちがふ拍子有。
或ハ、商の道、
分限になる拍子、分限にても其絶拍子、
道々につけて、拍子の相違有事也。
物毎、さかゆる拍子、おとろふる拍子、
能々分別すべし
兵法の拍子におゐて、さま／＼有事也。
先、あふ拍子をしつて、ちがふ拍子をわきまへ、
大小遅速の拍子のうちにも、
あたる拍子をしり、間の拍子をしり、
背く拍子をしる事、兵法の専也。
此背く拍子、わきまへ得ずしてハ、
兵法たしかならざる事也。
兵法の戦に、其敵々の拍子をしり、
敵の思ひよらざる拍子を以て、空の拍子をしり、
知恵の拍子より発して勝所也。
いづれの巻にも、拍子の事を専書記す也。
其書付を吟味して、能々鍛練有べきもの也。

Timing in strategy

There is timing in everything. Timing in strategy cannot be mastered without a great deal of practice.

Timing is important in dancing and pipe or string music, for they are in rhythm only if timing is good. Timing and rhythm are also involved in the military arts, shooting bows and guns, and riding horses. In all skills and abilities there is timing. There is also timing in the Void.

There is timing in the whole life of the warrior, in his thriving and declining, in his harmony and discord. Similarly, there is timing in the Way of the merchant, in the rise and fall of capital. All things entail rising and falling timing. You must be able to discern this. In strategy, there are various timing considerations. From the outset, you must know the applicable timing and the inapplicable timing, and from among the large and small things and the fast and slow timings find the relevant timing, first seeing the distance timing and the background timing. This is the main thing in strategy. It is especially important to know the background timing, otherwise your strategy will become uncertain.

You win in battles with the timing in the Void born of the timing of cunning by knowing the enemies' timing, and thus using a timing which the enemy does not expect.

All the five books are chiefly concerned with timing. You must train sufficiently to appreciate all this.

右、一流の兵法の道、
（朝な／＼夕な／＼勤おこなふに依て、
おのづから廣き心になつて）
多分一分の兵法として、世に傳る所、
始て書顕す事、地水火風空、是五巻也。
我兵法を学んと思ふ人ハ、道をおこなふ法あり。
第一に、よこしまになき事をおもふ所。
第二に、道の鍛錬する所。

第三に、諸藝にさハる所。
第四に、諸職の道を知事。
第五に、物毎の損徳をわきまゆる事。
第六に、諸事目利をしおぼゆる事。
第七に、目にみへぬ所をさとつて知事。
第八に、わずかなる事にも気を付る事。
第九に、役に立ぬ事をせざる事。

If you practise day and night in the above Ichi school strategy, your spirit will naturally broaden. In this manner, large-scale strategy and the strategy of hand-to-hand combat is propagated in the world. This is recorded for the first time in the five books of Ground, Water, Fire, Tradition (Wind) and Void. This is the Way for men who want to learn my strategy:

1. Do not think dishonestly.
2. The Way is in training.
3. Become acquainted with every art.
4. Know the Ways of all professions.
5. Distinguish between gain and loss in worldly matters.
6. Develop intuitive judgement and understanding for everything.
7. Perceive those things which cannot be seen.
8. Pay attention even to trifles.
9. Do nothing which is of no use.

大かた、かくのごとくの利を心にかけて、
兵法の道鍛練すべき也。
此道にかぎつて、直なる所を、廣く見立ざれば、
兵法の達者とはなりがたし。
此法を学び得てハ、一身にして、
二十三十の敵にもまくべき道にあらず。
先、氣に兵法をたへさず、直なる道を勤てハ、
手にてうち勝、目にみる事も人に勝、
又、鍛練を以て、惣躰自由なれば、
身にても人に勝、又、
此道になれたる心なれば、
心を以ても人に勝。此所に至てハ、
いかにとして、人に負道あらんや。
又、大なる兵法にしてハ、
善人をもつ事に勝、人数をつかふ事に勝、
身をたゞしくおこなふ道に勝、
国をおさむる事に勝、民をやしなふ事に勝、
世のれいほうをおこなふ（事）に勝。
いづれの道におゐても、人にまけざる所をしりて、
身をたすけ、名をたすくる所、
是兵法の道也。

It is important to start by setting these broad principles in your heart, and train in the Way of strategy. If you do not look at things on a large scale it will be difficult for you to master strategy. If you learn and attain this strategy you will never lose even to twenty or thirty enemies. More than anything to start with you must set your heart on strategy and earnestly stick to the Way. You will come to be able actually to beat men in fights, and win with your eye. Also by training you will be able to control your own body freely, conquer men with your body, and with sufficient training you will be able to beat ten men with your spirit. When you have reached this point, will it not mean that you are invincible?

Moreover, in large-scale strategy the superior man will manage many subordinates dexterously, bear himself correctly, govern the country and foster the people, thus preserving the ruler's discipline. If there is a Way involving the spirit of not being defeated, to help oneself and gain honour, it is the Way of strategy.

水之巻

Chapter 2

THE WATER BOOK

兵法二天一流の心、
水を本として、利方の法をおこなふに依て、
水之巻として、一流の太刀筋、
此書に書顕すもの也。
此道、何れもこまやかに
心のまゝにハ書分がたし。
たとへ言葉ハつゞかざると云とも、
利ハおのづから聞ゆべし。
此書に書付たる所、
一こと／＼、一字／＼にて思案すべし。
大かたに思ひてハ、
道の違ふ事多かるべし。
兵法の利におゐてハ、
一人と一人との勝負の様に書付たる所なりとも、
万人と万人との合戦の利に心得、
大に見立る所、肝要也。
此道にかぎつて、すこしなりとも道を違、
道の迷ひ有てハ、悪道におつるもの也。
此書付斗を見て、兵法の道に及事にハあらず。
此書に書付たるを、我身にとつて、
書付を見るとおもはず、習とおもはず、
にせものにせずして、
則、我心より見出したる利にして、
常に其身に成て、能々工夫すべし。

The spirit of the Niten Ichi school of strategy is based on water, and this Water Book explains methods of victory as the long-sword form of the Ichi school. Language does not extend to explaining the Way in detail, but it can be grasped intuitively. Study this book; read a word then ponder on it. If you interpret the meaning loosely, you will mistake the Way.

The principles of strategy are written down here in terms of single combat, but you must think broadly so that you attain an understanding for ten-thousand-a-side battles.

Strategy is different from other things in that if you mistake the Way even a little you will become bewildered and fall into bad ways.

If you merely read this book you will not reach the Way of strategy. Absorb the things written in this book. Do not just read, memorize or imitate, but study hard so that you realize the principle from within your own heart and absorb these things into your body.

兵法、心持の事

兵法の道におゐて、心の持様ハ、
常の心に替る事なかれ。
常にも兵法のときにも、少も替らずして、
心を廣く直にして、
きつくひつぱらず、すこしもたるまず、
心のかたよらぬやうに、心をまん中に置て、
心を静にゆるがせて、其ゆるぎのせつなも、
ゆるぎやまぬやうに、能々吟味すべし。
静なるときも、こゝろハしづかならず、
何と早き時も、心ハ少もはやからず。
心ハ躰につれず、躰ハ心につれず、
心に用心して、身には用心をせず。
心のたらぬ事なくして、心を少もあまらせず、
上の心はよハくとも、底の心を強く、
心を人に見分けられざる様にして、
少身なるものハ、心に大なる事を残らず知り、
大身なるものハ、心にちいさき事を能知りて、
大身も小身も、心を直にして、我身の

ひいきをせざる様に、心をもつ事肝要也。
心の内にごらず、廣くして、
廣き所に智恵をおくべき也。
智恵も心も、ひたとみがく事専也。
智恵をとぎ、天下の利非をわきまへ、
物毎の善悪をしり、
万の藝能、其道々をわたり、
世間の人にすこしもだまされざるやうにして、
後、兵法の智恵となる心也。
兵法の智恵にをゐて、
とりわきちがふ事、有もの也。
戦の場、万事せわしき時なりとも、
兵法、道理を極め、うごきなき心、
能々吟味すべし。

Spiritual bearing in strategy

In strategy, your spiritual bearing must not be any different from normal. Both in fighting and in everyday life you should be determined though calm. Meet the situation without tenseness yet not recklessly, your spirit settled yet unbiased. Even when your spirit is calm do not let your body relax, and when your body is relaxed do not let your spirit slacken. Do not let your spirit be influenced by your body, or your body influenced by your spirit. Be neither insufficiently spirited nor over-spirited. An elevated spirit is weak and a low spirit is weak. Do not let the enemy see your spirit.

Small people must be completely familiar with the spirit of large people, and large people must be familiar with the spirit of small people. Whatever your size, do not be misled by the reactions of your own body. With your spirit open and unconstricted, look at things from a high point of view. You must cultivate your wisdom and spirit. Polish your wisdom: learn public justice, distinguish between good and evil, study the Ways of different arts one by one. When you cannot be deceived by men you will have realized the wisdom of strategy.

The wisdom of strategy is different from other things. On the battlefield, even when you are hard-pressed, you should ceaselessly research the principles of strategy so that you can develop a steady spirit.

兵法、身なりの事

身のかゝり、顔ハうつむかず、あをのかず、
かたむかず、ひずまず、
目をミださず、額にしわをよせず、
眉あひにしわをよせて、
目の玉のうごかざる様にして、
またゝきをせぬやうに思ひて、
目を少しすくめる様にして、うらやかにみゆる顔。
鼻筋直にして、少おとがひに出す心也。
首ハ、うしろのすぢを直に、うなじに力をいれて、
肩より惣身はひとしく覚え、
両の肩をさげ、背筋をろくに、尻を出さず、
膝より足先まで力を入て、
腰のかゞまざるやうに、腹をはり、
くさびをしむると云て、脇ざしのさやに
腹をもたせて、帯のくつろがざる様に、
くさびをしむる、と云おしへ有。
惣而、兵法の身におゐて、常の身を兵法の身とし、
兵法の身を常の身とする事、肝要也。
能々吟味すべし。

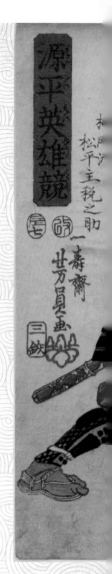

Stance in strategy

Adopt a stance with the head erect, neither hanging down, nor looking up, nor twisted. Your forehead and the space between your eyes should not be wrinkled. Do not roll your eyes nor allow them to blink, but slightly narrow them. With your features composed, keep the line of your nose straight with a feeling of slightly flaring your nostrils. Hold the line of the rear of the neck straight: instil vigour into your hairline, and in the same way from the shoulders down through your entire body. Lower both shoulders and, without the buttocks jutting out, put strength into your legs from the knees to the tops of your toes. Brace your abdomen so that you do not bend at the hips. Wedge your companion sword in your belt against your abdomen, so that your belt is not slack – this is called 'wedging in'.

In all forms of strategy, it is necessary to maintain the combat stance in everyday life and to make your everyday stance your combat stance. You must research this well.

兵法の眼付と云事

目の付様ハ、大に廣く付る目なり。
觀見二ツの事、
觀の目強く、見の目弱く、
遠き所をちかく見、近き所を遠く見る事、
兵法の専也。
敵の太刀を知り、聊敵の太刀を見ずと云事、
兵法の大事也。工夫有べし。
此目付、ちいさき兵法にも、
大なる兵法にも、おなじ事也。
目の玉うごかずして、
両脇を見る事、肝要也。
かやうの事、いそがしき時、
俄にハわきまへがたし。
此書付を覚、常住此目付になりて、
何事にも目付のかはらざる所、
能々吟味有べきもの也。

The gaze in strategy

The gaze should be large and broad. This is the twofold gaze, 'perception and sight'. Perception is strong and sight is weak.

In strategy, it is important to see distant things as if they were close and to take a distanced view of close things. It is important in strategy to know the enemy's sword and not to be distracted by insignificant movements of his sword. You must study this. The gaze is the same for single combat and for large-scale combat.

It is necessary in strategy to be able to look to both sides without moving the eyeballs. You cannot master this ability quickly. Learn what is written here; use this gaze in everyday life and do not vary it whatever happens.

太刀の持様の事

刀のとりやうハ、
大指、ひとさし（指）をうくるこゝろにもち、
たけ高指しめずゆるまず、
くすしゆび、小指をしむる心にして持也。
手のうちにはくつろぎの有事悪し。
敵をきるものなりとおもひて、太刀を取べし。
敵を切ときも、手の内にかハりなく、
手のすくまざる様に持べし。
若、敵の太刀を、はる事、うくる事、
あたる事、おさゆる事ありとも、
大指、人さしゆびばかりを、すこしかゆる心にして、
兎にも角にも切とおもひて、太刀を取べし。
ためし物など切ときの手のうちも、
兵法にしてきる時の手のうちも、
人をきるといふ手のうちにかハる事なし。
惣而、太刀にても手にても、いつくと云事を嫌ふ。
いつくハ、しぬる手也。いつかざるハ、いくる手也。
能々心得べきもの也。

Holding the long sword

Grip the long sword with a rather floating feeling in your thumb and forefinger, with the middle finger neither tight nor slack, and with the last two fingers tight. It is bad to have play in your hands.

When you take up a sword, you must feel intent on cutting the enemy. As you cut an enemy you must not change your grip, and your hands must not 'cower'. When you dash the enemy's sword aside, or ward it off, or force it down, you must slightly change the feeling in your thumb and forefinger. Above all, you must be intent on cutting the enemy in the way you grip the sword.

The grip for combat and for sword-testing[21] is the same. There is no such thing as a 'man-cutting grip'.

Generally, I dislike fixedness in both long swords and hands. Fixedness means a dead hand. Pliability is a living hand. You must bear this in mind.

足つかひの事

足のはこび様の事、つまさきをすこしうけて、
くびすをつよく踏べし。
足つかひハ、ことによりて、
大小遅速は有とも、常にあゆむがごとし。
足に、飛足、浮足、ふみすゆる足とて、
是三つ、嫌ふ足也。
此道の大事にいはく、
陰陽の足と云、是肝心也。
陰陽の足ハ、片足ばかりうごかさぬもの也。
切とき、引とき、うくる時迄も、
陰陽とて、右左／＼と踏足也。
かへす／＼、片足踏事有べからず。

Footwork[22]

With the tips of your toes somewhat floating, tread firmly with your heels. Whether you move fast or slow, with large or small steps, your feet must always move as in normal walking. I dislike the three walking methods known as 'jumping-foot', 'floating-foot' and 'fixed-steps'.

So-called 'Yin-Yang foot' is important to the Way. Yin-Yang foot means not moving on only one foot. It means moving your feet left-right and right-left when cutting, withdrawing, or warding off a cut. You should not move on one foot preferentially.

五方の構の事

五方の構ハ、上段、中段、下段、
右の脇に構る事、左の脇に構る事、
是五方也。
構五ツにわかつといへども、
皆人を切らむため也。
構、五ツより外ハなし。
何れの構なりとも、構ると思はず、
切事なりと思ふべし。
構の大小は、ことにより、利にしたがふべし。
上中下ハ、躰の構也。両脇ハ、ゆふの構也。
右左のかまへ、上のつまりて、
脇一方つまりたる所などにての構也。
右左ハ、所によりて分別有。
此道の大事にいはく、
構の極は中段と心得べし。
中段、かまへの本意也。
兵法大にして見よ、中段は大将の座也。
大将につぎ、跡四段の構也。
能々吟味すべし。

The Five Attitudes

The Five Attitudes are: Upper, Middle, Lower, Right Side and Left Side. These are the five. Although attitude has these five dimensions, the one purpose of all of them is to cut the enemy. There are none but these five attitudes.

Whatever attitude you are in, do not be conscious of making the attitude; think only of cutting. Your attitude should be large or small according to the situation. Upper, Lower and Middle attitudes are decisive. Left Side and Right Side attitudes are fluid. Left and Right attitudes should be used if there is an obstruction overhead or to one side. The decision to use Left or Right depends on the place.

    The essence of the Way is this. To understand attitude, you must thoroughly understand the Middle attitude. The Middle attitude is the heart of the attitudes. If we look at strategy on a broad scale, the Middle attitude is the seat of the commander, with the other four attitudes following the commander. You must appreciate this.

太刀の道と云事

太刀の道を知ると云ハ、
常に我さす刀を、指二つにて振る時も、
道筋よくしりてハ、自由に振もの也。
太刀をはやくふらんとするによつて、
太刀の道さかひて振がたし。
太刀ハ、振よきほどに、静に振心也。
或は扇、或は小刀などつかふ様に、
はやくふらんとおもふに依て、
太刀の道違ひて振がたし。
夫ハ、小刀きざみといひて、
太刀にてハ人のきれざるもの也。
太刀を打さげてハ、あげよき道へ上、
横にふりてハ、横にもどりよき道へもどし、
いかにも大にひぢをのべて、
強く振る事、是太刀の道也。
我が兵法の五つの表をつかひ覚ゆれバ、
太刀の道定て振よき所也。
能々鍛錬すべし。

The Way of the long sword

Knowing the Way of the long sword[23] means we can wield with two fingers the sword we usually carry. If we know the path of the sword well, we can wield it easily. If you try to wield the long sword quickly, you will mistake the Way. To wield the long sword well you must wield it calmly. If you try to wield it quickly, like a folding fan[24] or a short sword, you will err by using 'short sword chopping'. You cannot cut a man with a long sword using this method.

When you have cut downwards with the long sword, lift it straight upwards; when you cut sideways, return the sword along a sideways path. Return the sword in a reasonable way, always stretching the elbows broadly. Wield the sword strongly.

This is the Way of the long sword.

If you learn to use the five approaches of my strategy, you will be able to wield a sword well. You must train constantly.

五つの表の次第の事

第一の構、中段。
敵に行相時、太刀先を敵のかほへ付て、
敵太刀うちかくる時、右へ太刀をはづしてのり、
又敵うち懸る時、切先かへしにて打、
うち落したる太刀、其まゝ置、
又敵の打かくる時、下より敵の手をはる、
是第一也

惣別、此五つの表、
書付る斗にてハ合点なりがたし。
五ツの表の分ハ、
手にとつて、太刀の道稽古する所也。
此五つの太刀筋にて、
我太刀の道をもしり、
いかやうにも敵のうつ太刀しるゝ所也。
是、二刀の太刀の構、五つより外にあらず、と
しらする所也。

The Five Approaches

1. The first approach is the Middle attitude. Confront the enemy with the point of your sword against his face. When he attacks, dash his sword to the right and 'ride' it. Or, when the enemy attacks, deflect the point of his sword by hitting downwards, keeping your long sword where it is, and as the enemy renews the attack cut his arms from below. This is the first method. The five approaches are this kind of thing. You must train repeatedly using a long sword in order to learn them. When you master my Way of the long sword, you will be able to control any attack the enemy makes. I assure you, there are no attitudes other than the five attitudes of the long sword of Ni To.

一　表、第二の次第の事。
第二の太刀、上段に構、
敵打懸る所、一度に敵を打也。
敵を打はづしたる太刀、其まゝ置て、
又敵のうつところを、下よりすくひ上てうつ。
今一つうつも、同じ事也

此表の内におゐてハ、
様々の心持、色々の拍子、
此表の内を以て、一流の鍛錬をすれバ、
五つの太刀の道、こまやかにしつて、
いかやうにも勝所有。稽古すべき也。

一　表、第三の次第の事。
第三の構、下段にもち、ひつさげたる心にして、
敵のうちかくる所を、下より手をはるなり。
手をはる所を、又敵はる太刀を
打落さんとする所を、こす拍子にて、
敵うちたる跡、二のうでを横に切こゝろ也。
下段にて、敵のうつ所を、
一度に打とむる事也。
下段の構、道をはこぶに、
はやき時もおそき時も、出合もの也。
太刀をとつて、鍛錬すべきもの也。

2. In the second approach with the long sword, from the Upper attitude cut the enemy just as he attacks. If the enemy evades the cut, keep your sword where it is and, scooping from below, cut him as he renews the attack. It is possible to repeat the cut from here.

In this method, there are various changes in timing and spirit. You will be able to understand this by training in the Ichi school. You will always win with the five long sword methods. You must train repeatedly.

3. In the third approach, adopt the Lower attitude, anticipating scooping up. When the enemy attacks, hit his hands from below. As you do so, he may try to hit your sword down. If this is the case, cut his upper arm(s) horizontally with a feeling of 'crossing'. This means that from the Lower attitudes you hit the enemy at the instant that he attacks.

You will encounter this method often, both as a beginner and in later strategy. You must train holding a long sword.

一　表、第四の次第の事。
第四の構、左の脇に横にかまへて、
敵のうち懸る手を、下よりはるべし。
下よりはるを、敵うち落さんとするを、
手をはる心にて、其ま〻太刀の道をうけ、
わが肩の上へ、すぢかひにきるべし。

一　表、第五の次第の事。
第五の（次第、太刀の）構、
わが右のわきに横に構て、
敵うち懸る所の位をうけ、
我太刀の下の横より筋違て、上段に振あげ、
上より直にきるべし。
これも太刀の道よくしらんため也。
此表にてふりつけぬれバ、
おもき太刀自由にふらる〻所也。

此五つの表におゐて、こまかに書付る事に非ず。
我家の一通、太刀の道をしり、
又、大かた拍子をもおぼへ、敵の太刀を見分事、
先、此五つにて、不断手をからす所也。
敵と戦のうちにも、此太刀筋をからして、
敵の心をうけ、いろ／＼の拍子にて、
如何やうにも勝所也。能々分別すべし。

4. In this fourth approach, adopt the Left Side attitude. As the enemy attacks, hit his hands from below. If, as you hit his hands, he attempts to dash down your sword, with the feeling of hitting his hands, parry the path of his long sword and cut across from above your shoulder.

5. In the fifth approach, the sword is in the Right Side attitude. In accordance with the enemy's attack, cross your sword from below at the side to the Upper attitude. Then cut straight from above. This method is essential for knowing the Way of the long sword well. If you can use this method, you can freely wield a heavy long sword.

I cannot describe in detail how to use these five approaches. You must become well acquainted with my 'in harmony with the long sword' Way, learn large-scale timing, understand the enemy's long sword, and become used to the five approaches from the outset. You will always win by using these five methods, with various timing considerations discerning the enemy's spirit. You must consider all this carefully.

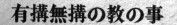

有構無構の教の事

有構無構と云ハ、
太刀を構と云事、有べき事にあらず。
されども、五方に置事あれバ、
構ともなるべし。
太刀は、敵の縁により、
所により、けいきにしたがひ、
いづれのかたに置たりとも、
其敵きりよき様に持心也。
上段も、時に随ひ、
少さぐる心なれバ、中段となり、
中段も、利により少上れば、上段となる。
下段も、折にふれ少上れバ、中段となる。
両脇の構も、位により、少し中へ出せバ、
中段、下段ともなる心也。
然によつて、構ハ有て構ハなきと云利也。

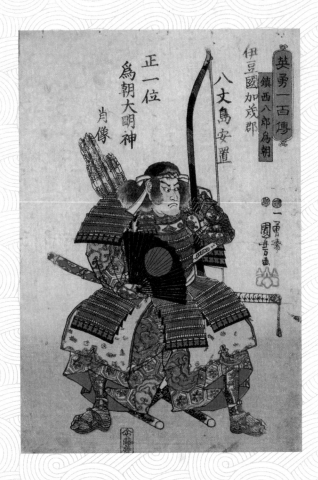

The Attitude-No-Attitude teaching

Attitude-No-Attitude means that there is no need for what are known as long sword attitudes.

Even so, attitudes exist as the five ways of holding the long sword. However you hold the sword, it must be in such a way that it is easy to cut the enemy well, in accordance with the situation, the place, and your relation to the enemy. From the Upper attitude, as your spirit lessens you can adopt the Middle attitude, and from the Middle attitude you can raise the sword a little in your technique and adopt the Upper attitude. From the Lower attitude, you can raise the sword a little and adopt the Middle attitudes as the occasion demands. According to the situation, if you turn your sword from either the Left Side or Right Side attitude towards the centre, the Middle or the Lower attitude results.

The principle of this is called 'Existing Attitude – Non-existing Attitude'.

先、太刀をとりてハ、
何れにしてなりとも敵をきる、と云心也。
若、敵のきる太刀を、うくる、はる、
あたる、ねばる、さはる、
など云事あれども、
みな敵をきる縁也、と心得べし。
うくるとおもひ、はるとおもひ、
あたるとおもひ、ねばるとおもひ、
さはると思ふによつて、切事不足なるべし。
何事もきる縁とおもふ事、肝要也。
能々吟味すべし。
兵法大にして、人数だてと云も構也。
ミな合戦に勝縁也。
いつくと云事悪し。能々工夫すべし。

The primary thing when you take a sword in your hands is your intention to cut the enemy, whatever the means. Whenever you parry, hit, spring, strike or touch the enemy's cutting sword, you must cut the enemy in the same movement. It is essential to attain this. If you think only of hitting, springing, striking or touching the enemy, you will not be able actually to cut him. More than anything, you must be thinking of carrying your movement through to cutting him. You must thoroughly research this.

Attitude in strategy on a larger scale is called 'battle array'. Such attitudes are all for winning battles. Fixed formation is bad. Study this well.

敵をうつに、一拍子の打の事

敵を打拍子に、一拍子と云て、
敵我あたるほどの位を得て、
敵のわきまへぬうちを心に得て、
我身もうごかさず、心もつけず、
いかにも早く、直にうつ拍子也。
敵の、太刀ひかん、はづさん、うたん、
とおもふ心のなきうちを打拍子、是一拍子也。
此拍子、よくならひ得て、
間の拍子をはやく打事、鍛錬すべし。

二のこしの拍子の事

二のこしの拍子、我うちださんとするとき、
敵はやく引、はやくはりのくる様なる時ハ、
我うつとみせて、敵のはりてたるむ所を打、
引てたるむところをうつ、
これ二のこしの拍子也。
此書付ばかりにてハ、中々打得がたかるべし。
おしへをうけてハ、忽合点のゆく所也。

To hit the enemy 'in one timing'

'In one timing' means, when you have closed with the enemy, to hit him as quickly and directly as possible, without moving your body or settling your spirit, while you see that he is still undecided. The timing of hitting before the enemy decides to withdraw, break or hit, is this 'in one timing'.

You must train to achieve this timing, to be able to hit in the timing of an instant.

The 'abdomen timing of two'

When you attack and the enemy quickly retreats, as you see him tense you must feint a cut. Then, as he relaxes, follow up and hit him. This is the 'abdomen timing of two'.

It is very difficult to attain this merely by reading this book, but you will soon understand with a little instruction.

無念無相の打と云事

敵もうち出さんとし、我も打だ さんとおもふとき、
身もうつ身になり、心も打心になつて、
手ハ、いつとなく、空より後ばやに強く打事、
是無念無相とて、一大事の打也。
此打、たび／＼出合打也。
能々ならひ得て、鍛錬有べき儀也。

'No design, no conception'[25]

In this method, when the enemy attacks and you also decide to attack, hit with your body, and hit with your spirit, and hit from the Void with your hands, accelerating strongly. This is the 'no design, no conception' cut.

This is the most important method of hitting. It is often used. You must train hard to understand it.

流水の打と云事

流水の打と云て、敵あひに成て、せりあふ時、
敵、はやくひかん、はやくはづさん、
早く太刀をはりのけんとする時、
我身も心も大になつて、
太刀を、我身の跡より、
いかほどもゆる／＼と、
よどミの有様に、大に強くうつ事也。
此打、ならひ得てハ、たしかにうちよきもの也。
敵の位を見分事、肝要也。

縁のあたりと云事

我うち出す時、
敵、打とめん、はりのけんとする時、
我打一つにして、あたまをも打、
手をも打、足をも打。太刀の道ひとつをもつて、
いづれなりとも打所、是縁の打也。
此打、能々打ならひ（得てハ）、何時も出合打也。
さい／＼打合て、分別有べき事也。

石火のあたりと云事

石火のあたりハ、
敵の太刀とわが太刀と付合程にて、
我太刀少もあげずして、いかにも強く打也。
是ハ、足もつよく、身も強く、手も強く、
三所をもつて、はやく打べき也。
此打、たび／＼打ならはずしてハ、打がたし。
能鍛錬をすれバ、つよくあたるもの也。

The 'flowing water' cut

The 'flowing water' cut is used when you are struggling blade to blade with the enemy. When he breaks and quickly withdraws, trying to spring with his long sword, expand your body and spirit and cut him as slowly as possible with your long sword, following your body like stagnant water. You can cut with certainty if you learn this. You must discern the enemy's grade.

The 'continuous' cut

When you attack and the enemy also attacks and your swords spring together, in one action cut his head, hands and legs. When you cut several places with one sweep of the long sword, it is the 'continuous' cut. You must practise this cut; it is often used. With detailed practice you should be able to understand it.

The 'fire and stones' cut

The 'fire and stones' cut means that when the enemy's long sword and your long sword clash together, you cut as strongly as possible without raising the sword even a little. This means cutting quickly with the hands, body and legs – all three cutting strongly. If you train well enough you will be able to strike strongly.

紅葉の打と云事

紅葉のうち、敵の太刀を打落し、
太刀とりはなす（はなつ）心也。
敵、前に太刀を構、
うたん、はらん、うけんと思ふ時、
我打心ハ、無念無相の打、
又、石火の打にても、敵の太刀を強く打、
其まゝ跡をはねる心にて、切先さがりにうてバ、
敵の太刀、かならず落もの也。
この打、鍛練すれバ、打落す事安し。
能々稽古有べし。

The 'red leaves' cut

The 'red leaves' cut (alluding to falling, dying leaves) means knocking down the enemy's long sword. The spirit should be getting control of his sword. When the enemy is in a long-sword attitude in front of you and intent on cutting, hitting and parrying, you strongly hit the enemy's sword with the 'fire and stones' cut, perhaps in the design of the 'no design, no conception' cut. If you then beat down the point of his sword with a sticky feeling, he will necessarily drop the sword. If you practise this cut, it becomes easy to make the enemy drop his sword. You must train repetitively.

太刀にかはる身と云事

身にかはる太刀とも云べし。
惣而、敵をうつ身に、
太刀も身も一度にハうたざるもの也。
敵の打縁により、
身をバさきに打身になり、
太刀ハ、身にかまはず打所也。
若ハ、身はゆかず、太刀にてうつ事はあれども、
大かたハ、身を先へ打、太刀を跡より打もの也。
能々吟味して、打習べき也。

打とあたると云事

うつと云事、あたると云事、二つ也。
うつと云こゝろハ、何れのうちにても、
おもひうけて、たしかに打也。
あたるハ、行あたるほどの心にて、
何と強くあたり、忽敵の死ぬるほどにても、
これハ、あたる也。
打と云ハ、心得て打所也。吟味すべし。
敵の手にても、足にても、
あたると云ハ、先、あたる也。
あたりて後を、強くうたんため也。
あたるハ、さはるほどの心、
能ならひ得てハ、各別の事也。
工夫すべし。

The 'body in place of the long sword'

Also the 'long sword in place of the body'. Usually we move the body and the sword at the same time to cut the enemy. However, according to the enemy's cutting method, you can dash against him with your body first, and afterwards cut with the sword. If his body is immovable, you can cut first with the long sword, but generally you hit first with the body and then cut with the long sword. You must research this well and practise hitting.

'Cut and slash'

To 'cut and slash' are two different things. Cutting, whatever form of cutting it is, is decisive, with a resolute spirit. Slashing is nothing more than touching the enemy. Even if you slash strongly, and even if the enemy dies instantly, it is slashing. When you cut, your spirit is resolved. You must appreciate this. If you first slash the enemy's hands or legs, you must then cut strongly. Slashing is in spirit the same as touching. When you realize this, they become indistinguishable. Learn this well.

しうこうの身と云事

秋猴の身とハ、手を出さぬ心也。
敵へ入身に、少も手を出だす心なく、
敵打つ前、身をはやく入心也。
手を出さんとおもへバ、
かならず身の遠のく物なるによつて、
惣身をはやくうつり入心也。
手にてうけ合する程の間にハ、
身も入安きもの也。
能々吟味すべし。

しつかうの身と云事

漆膠とハ、入身に、よく付て離ぬ心也。
敵の身に入とき、かしらをも付、身をも付、
足をも付、強く付所也。
人毎、顔足ハ早くいれども、
身ハのくもの也。
敵の身へ我身をよく付、
少も身のあひのなき様に、つくもの也。
能々吟味有べし。

'Chinese monkey's body'

The 'Chinese monkey's body' is the spirit of not stretching out your arms. The spirit is to get in quickly, without in the least extending your arms, before the enemy cuts. If you are intent upon not stretching out your arms, you are effectively far away; the spirit is to go in with your whole body. When you come to within arm's reach it becomes easy to move your body in. You must research this well.

'Glue and lacquer emulsion body'[26]

The spirit of 'glue and lacquer emulsion body' is to stick to the enemy and not separate from him. When you approach the enemy, stick firmly with your head, body and legs. People tend to advance their head and legs quickly, but their body lags behind. You should stick firmly so that there is not the slightest gap between the enemy's body and your body. You must consider this carefully.

たけくらべと云事

たけくらべと云ハ、いづれにても敵へ入こむ時、
我身のちゞまざる様にして、
足をも延べ、腰をものべ、首をも延て、強く入り、
敵のかほと顔とならべ、身のたけをくらぶるに、
くらべ勝と思ほど、たけ高くなつて、
強く入所、肝心也。能々工夫有べし。

ねばりをかくると云事

敵も打かけ、我も太刀うちかくるに、
敵うくる時、我太刀、敵の太刀に付て、
ねばる心にして入也。
ねばるハ、太刀はなれがたき心、
あまり強くなき心に入べし。
敵の太刀に付て、ねばりをかけ、入ときハ、
いかほど静に入ても、くるしからず。
ねばると云事と、もつるゝと云事、
ねばるハ強し、もつるゝハ弱し。
此事分別有べし。

身のあたりと云事

身のあたりハ、敵のきはへ入込て、
身にて敵にあたる心也。
すこし我顔をそばめ、わが左の肩を出し、
敵の胸にあたる也。
我身を、いかほども強くなり、あたる事、

いきあひ拍子にて、はづむ心に入べし。
此入事、入ならひ得てハ、
敵二間も三間もはけのく程、強きもの也。
敵死入ほども、あたる也。
能々鍛錬有べし。

'To strive for height'

By 'to strive for height' is meant, when you close with the enemy, to strive with him for superior height without cringing. Stretch your legs, stretch your hips, and stretch your neck face to face with him. When you think you have won, and you are the higher, thrust in strongly. You must learn this.

'To apply stickiness'

When the enemy attacks and you also attack with the long sword, you should go in with a sticky feeling and fix your long sword against the enemy's as you receive his cut. The spirit of stickiness is not hitting very strongly, but hitting so that the long swords do not separate easily. It is best to approach as calmly as possible when hitting the enemy's long sword with stickiness. The difference between 'stickiness' and 'entanglement' is that stickiness is firm and entanglement is weak. You must appreciate this.

The 'body strike'

The 'body strike' means to approach the enemy through a gap in his guard. The spirit is to strike him with your body. Turn your face a little aside and strike the enemy's breast with your left shoulder thrust out. Approach with a spirit of bouncing the enemy away, striking as strongly as possible in time with your breathing. If you achieve this method of closing with the enemy, you will be able to knock him ten or twenty feet away. It is possible to strike the enemy until he is dead. Train well.

義士忠臣鑑

竹林定七隆重

一筆菴誌

應需

一勇齋國芳画

清

三つのうけの事

三のうけと云ハ、敵へ入込時、
敵うち出す太刀をうくるに、
我太刀にて、敵の目をつく様にして、
敵の太刀を、わが右のかたへ
引ながしてうくる事。
又、つきうけと云て、敵の打太刀を、
敵の右の目をつく様にして、
くびをはさむ心に、つきかけてうくる所。
又、敵の打時、みじかき太刀にて入に、
うくる太刀ハ、さのみかまハず、
我左の手にて、敵のつらをつく様にして入込。
是三つのうけ也。左の手をにぎりて、
こぶしにてつらをつく様に思ふべし。
能々鍛錬有べきもの也。

Three ways to parry his attack

There are three methods to parry a cut:

First, by dashing the enemy's long sword to your right, as if thrusting at his eyes, when he makes an attack;

Or to parry by thrusting the enemy's long sword towards his right eye with the feeling of snipping his neck;

Or, when you have a short 'long sword', without worrying about parrying the enemy's long sword, to close with him quickly, thrusting at his face with your left hand.

These are the three ways of parrying. You must bear in mind that you can always clench your left hand and thrust at the enemy's face with your fist. It is necessary to train well.

面をさすと云事

面をさすと云ハ、敵太刀相になりて、
敵の太刀の間、我太刀の間に、
敵のかほを、我太刀先にてつく心に
常におもふ所、肝心也。
敵の顔をつく心あれバ、
敵のかほ、身ものるもの也。
敵をのらするやうにしてハ、
色々勝所の利有。能々工夫すべし。
戦のうちに、敵の身のる心有てハ、はや勝所也。
それによつて、面をさすと云事、
忘るべからず。兵法稽古のうちに、
此利、鍛練有べきもの也。

心をさすと云事

心をさすと云ハ、戦のうちに、
上つまり、わきつまりたる所などにて、
切事いづれもなりがたきとき、敵をつく事、
敵の打太刀をはづす心ハ、
我太刀のむねを直に敵に見せて、
太刀先ゆがまざる様に引とりて、
敵の胸をつく事也。
若、我草臥たる時か、
又ハ刀のきれざる時などに、
此儀専用る心也。能々分別すべし。

'To stab at the face'

'To stab at the face' means, when you are in confrontation with the enemy, that your spirit is intent on stabbing at his face, following the line of the blades with the point of your long sword. If you are intent on stabbing at his face, his face and body will become rideable. When the enemy becomes rideable, there are various opportunities for winning. You must concentrate on this. When fighting and the enemy's body becomes as if rideable, you can win quickly, so you ought not to forget to stab at the face. You must pursue the value of this technique through training.

'To stab at the heart'

'To stab at the heart' means, when fighting and there are obstructions above or to the sides, and whenever it is difficult to cut, to thrust at the enemy. You must stab the enemy's breast without letting the point of your long sword waver, showing the enemy the ridge of the blade square-on, and with the spirit of deflecting his long sword. The spirit of this principle is often useful when we become tired or for some reason our long sword will not cut. You must understand the application of this method.

かつとつと云事

喝咄と云ハ、何れも
我うちかけ、敵をおつこむ時、
敵又打かへす様なる所、
下より敵をつく様にあげて、かへしにて打事、
いづれもはやき拍子をもつて、喝咄と打。
喝とつきあげ、咄と打心也。
此拍子、何時も打あいの内にハ、専出合事也。
喝咄のしやう、切先あぐる心にして、
敵をつくと思ひ、あぐると一度に打拍子、
能稽古して、吟味有べき事也。

はりうけと云事

はりうけと云ハ、敵と打合とき、
とたん／＼と云拍子になるに、
敵の打所を、我太刀にてはり合せ、うつ也。
はり合する心ハ、さのみきつくはるにあらず、
又、うくるにあらず。
敵の打太刀に應じて、打太刀をはりて、
はるよりはやく、敵を打事也。
はるにて先をとり、うつにて先をとる所、肝要也。
はる拍子能あへバ、敵何と強くうちても、
少はる心あれバ、太刀先の落る事にあらず。
能習得て、吟味有べし。

'To scold "Tut-TUT!"'

'Scold' means that, when the enemy tries to counter-cut as you attack, you counter-cut again from below as if thrusting at him, trying to hold him down. With very quick timing you cut, scolding the enemy. Thrust up, 'Tut!', and cut 'TUT!' This timing is encountered time and time again in exchanges of blows. The way to scold Tut-TUT is to time the cut simultaneously with raising your long sword as if to thrust the enemy. You must learn this through repetitive practice.

The 'smacking parry'

By 'smacking parry' is meant that when you clash swords with the enemy, you meet his attacking cut on your long sword with a tee-dum, tee-dum rhythm, smacking his sword and cutting him. The spirit of the smacking parry is not parrying, or smacking strongly, but smacking the enemy's long sword in accordance with his attacking cut, primarily intent on quickly cutting him. If you understand the timing of smacking, however hard your long swords clash together, your sword point will not be knocked back even a little. You must research sufficiently to realize this.

多敵の位の事

多敵のくらゐと云ハ、
一身にして大勢と戦ときの事也。
我刀脇指をぬきて、
左右へ廣く太刀を横に捨て、構る也。
敵は四方よりかゝるとも、
一方へおひまはす心也。
敵かゝる位、前後を見分て、
先へすゝむものにはやく行あひ、
大に目を付て、敵うち出す位を得て、
右の太刀も左の太刀も、一度に振ちがへて、
行太刀にて、其敵をきり、もどる太刀にて、
わきにすゝむ敵をきる心也。
太刀を振ちがへて待事悪し。
はやく両脇の位に構、敵の出たる所を、
強くきりこミ、おつくづして、其まゝ、
又敵の出たるかたへかゝり、振くづす心也。
いかにもして、敵をひとへに、
うをつなぎにおひなす心にしかけて、
敵のかさなるとミヘバ、
其まゝ間をすかさず、強くはらひこむべし。

太平記英勇傳
大多上總介平春永公

'There are many enemies'

'There are many enemies'[27] applies when you are fighting one against many. Draw both sword and companion sword and assume a wide-stretched left and right attitude. The spirit is to chase the enemies around from side to side, even though they come from all four directions. Observe their attacking order, and go to meet first those who attack first. Sweep your eyes around broadly, carefully examining the attacking order, and cut left and right alternately with your swords. Waiting is bad. Always quickly reassume your attitudes to both sides, cut the enemies down as they advance, crushing them in the direction from which they attack. Whatever you do, you must drive the enemy together, as if tying a line of fishes, and when they are seen to be piled up, cut them down strongly without giving them room to move.

打あひの利の事

此打あひの利と云事にて、
兵法、太刀にての勝利をわきまゆる所也。
こまやかに書記すにあらず。
（能）稽古有て、勝所を知べきもの也。
大かた、兵法の実の道を顕す太刀也。（口傳）

一つの打と云事

此一つの打と云心をもつて、
たしかに勝所を得事也。
兵法よく学ざれバ、心得がたし。
此儀、よく鍛錬すれバ、兵法心のまゝになつて、
おもうまゝに勝道也。能々稽古すべし。

The advantage when coming to blows

You can know how to win through strategy with the long sword, but it cannot be clearly explained in writing. You must practise diligently in order to understand how to win.

Oral tradition[28]: 'The true Way of strategy is revealed in the long sword.'

'One cut'

You can win with certainty with the spirit of 'one cut'. It is difficult to attain this if you do not learn strategy well. If you train well in this Way, strategy will come from your heart and you will be able to win at will. You must train diligently.

直通の位と云事

直通の心、二刀一流の實の道をうけて
傳ゆる所也。能々鍛練して、
此兵法に身をなす事、肝要也。(口傳)

兵法、太刀をとつて人に勝處を覚るハ、
先、五つの表を以て、五方の構をしり、
太刀の道を覚へて、惣躰やはらかになり、
心もきゝ出、道の拍子をしり、
おのれと太刀手さへて、
身も足も、心のまゝ、ほどけたる時に随ひ、
一人に勝、二人にかち、
兵法の善悪をしるほどになり、
此一書の内を、一ヶ条／＼と稽古して、
敵と戦ひ、次第／＼に道の利を得て、
たへず心にかけ、急ぐ心なくして、
折々手にふれ、徳を覚へ、
何れの人とも打あひ、其心をしつて、
千里の道も、ひと足宛はこぶ也。
ゆる／＼と思ひ、此法をおこなふ事、
武士の役なりと心得て、
今日ハ昨日の我に勝、あすハ下手に勝、
後ハ上手に勝と思ひ、此書物のごとくにして、
少もわきの道へ心のゆかざる様に思ふべし。
たとへ何ほどの敵に打勝ても、
習にそむく事におゐてハ、
實の道に有べからず。
此利、心にうかミてハ、一身をもつて、

数十人にも勝心のわきまへ有べし。
然上ハ、劒術の智力にて、
大分一分の兵法をも得道すべし。
千日の稽古を鍛とし、万日の稽古を錬とす。
能々吟味有べきもの也。

'Direct communication'

The spirit of 'direct communication' is how the true Way of the Nito Ichi school is received and handed down.

Oral tradition: 'Teach your body strategy.'

To learn how to win with the long sword in strategy, first learn the five approaches and the five attitudes, and absorb the Way of the long sword naturally in your body. You must understand spirit and timing, handle the long sword naturally, and move body and legs in harmony with your spirit. Whether beating one man or two, you will then know values in strategy.

Study the contents of this book, taking one item at a time, and through fighting with enemies you will gradually come to know the principle of the Way.

Deliberately, with a patient spirit, absorb the virtue of all this, from time to time raising your hand in combat. Maintain this spirit whenever you cross swords with an enemy.

Step by step walk the thousand-mile road.

Study strategy over the years and achieve the spirit of the warrior. Today is victory over yourself of yesterday; tomorrow is your victory over lesser men. Next, in order to beat more skilful men, train according to this book, not allowing your heart to be swayed along a side track. Even if you kill an enemy, if it is not based on what you have learned it is not the true Way.

If you attain this Way of victory, then you will be able to beat several tens of men. What remains is sword-fighting ability, which you can attain in battles and duels.

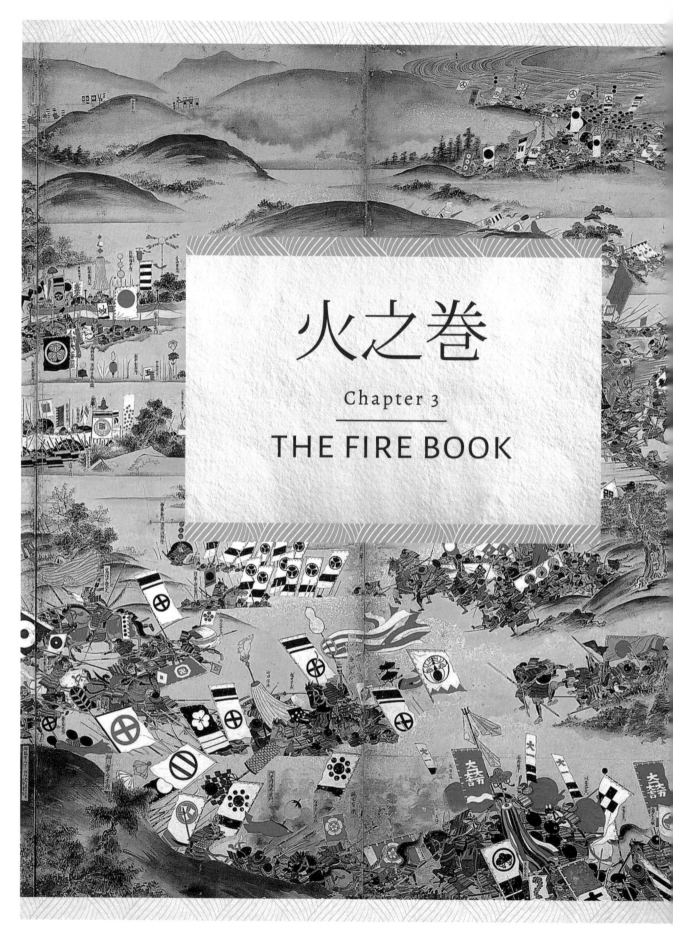

火之巻

Chapter 3

THE FIRE BOOK

二刀一流の兵法、戦の事を火に思ひとつて、
戦勝負の事を、火之巻として、
此巻に書顕す也。
先、世間の人毎に、兵法の利を
ちいさくおもひなして、或ハゆびさきにて、
手くび五寸三寸の利をしり、或ハ扇をとつて、
ひぢより先の先後のかちをわきまへ、
又ハしなひなどにて、わづかのはやき利を覚へ、
手をきかせならひ、足をきかせならひ、
少の利のはやき所を専とする事也。
我兵法におゐて、数度の勝負に、
一命をかけてうち合、生死二つの利をわけ、
刀の道を覚へ、敵の打太刀の強弱を知り、
刀のはむねの道をわきまへ、
敵をうちはたす所の鍛練を得るに、
ちいさき事、弱き事、思ひよらざる所也。
殊に六具かためてなどの利に、
ちいさき事、思ひいづる事にあらず。
されバ、命をはかりの打あひにおゐて、
一人して五人十人ともたゝかひ、
其勝道をたしかにしる事、我道の兵法也。
然によつて、一人して十人に勝、
千人をもつて万人に勝道理、
何のしやべつあらんや。能々吟味有べし。
さりなから、常／＼の稽古の時、
千人万人をあつめ、此道しならふ事、
なる事にあらず。獨太刀をとつても、
其敵／＼の智略をはかり、

敵の強弱、手だてを知り、兵法の智徳をもつて、
萬人に勝所をきはめ、此道の達者となり、
我兵法の直道、世界におゐて、たれか得ん、
又いづれかきはめんと、たしかに思ひとつて、
朝鍛夕錬して、みがきおほせて後、
獨自由を得、おのづから奇特を得、
通力不思儀有所、
是兵として法をおこなふ息也。

In this, the Fire Book of the Nito Ichi school of strategy, I describe fighting as fire.

In the first place, people think narrowly about the benefit of strategy. By using only their fingertips, they only know the benefit of three of the five inches of the wrist. They let a contest be decided, as with the folding fan, merely by the span of their forearms. They specialize in the small matter of dexterity, learning such trifles as hand and leg movements with the bamboo practice sword.[29]

In my strategy, the training for killing enemies is by way of many contests, fighting for survival, discovering the meaning of life and death, learning the Way of the sword, judging the strength of attacks and understanding the Way of the 'edge and ridge' of the sword.

You cannot profit from small techniques, particularly when full armour[30] is worn. My Way of strategy is the sure method to win when fighting for your life one man against five or ten. There is nothing wrong with the principle 'one man can beat ten, so a thousand men can beat ten thousand'. You must research this. Of course, you cannot assemble a thousand or ten thousand men for everyday training. But you can become a master of strategy by training alone with a sword, so that you can understand the enemy's strategies, his strength and resources, and come to appreciate how to apply strategy to beat ten thousand enemies.

Any man who wants to master the essence of my strategy must research diligently, training morning and evening. Thus can he polish his skill, become free from self, and realize extraordinary ability. He will come to possess miraculous power.

This is the practical result of strategy.

場の次第と云事

場の位を見分る所、場におゐて、
日をおふと云事有。
日をうしろになして搆る也。
若、所により、日をうしろにする事
ならざる時ハ、右の脇へ日をなす様にすべし。
座敷にても、あかりをうしろ、右わきとなす事、
同前也。うしろの場つまらざる様に、
左の場をくつろげ、右脇の場をつめて、
搆へたき事也。
よるにても、敵のミゆる所にてハ、
火をうしろにおひ、あかりを右脇にする事、
同前と心得て、搆べきもの也。
敵を見おろすと云て、
少も高き所に搆るやうに心得べし。
座敷にてハ、上座を高き所と思ふべし。
さて、戦になりて、敵を追まはす事、
我左のかたへ追まハす心、
難所を敵のうしろにさせ、
何れにても難所へ追かくる事、肝要也。
難所にて、敵に場をみせず、といひて、
敵にかほをふらせず、油断なくせりつむる心也。
座敷にても、敷居、鴨居、戸障子、椽など、
又、柱などの方へ、おひつむるにも、
場をみせずと云事、同前也。
いづれも敵を追懸る方、足場のわろき所、
又ハわきにかまひの有所、何れも場の徳を用て、
場の勝を得と云心専にして、
能々吟味し、鍛錬有べきもの也。

Depending on the place

Examine your environment.

Stand in the sun; that is, take up an attitude with the sun behind you. If the situation does not allow this, you must try to keep the sun on your right side. In buildings, you must stand with the entrance behind you or to your right. Make sure that your rear is unobstructed, and that there is free space on your left, your right side being occupied with your sword attitude. At night, if the enemy can be seen, keep the fire behind you and the entrance to your right, and otherwise take up your attitude as above. You must look down on the enemy, and take up your attitude on slightly higher places. For example, the Kamiza[31] in a house is thought of as a high place.

When the fight comes, always endeavour to chase the enemy around to your left side. Chase him towards awkward places, and try to keep him with his back to awkward places. When the enemy gets into an inconvenient position, do not let him look around, but conscientiously chase him around and pin him down. In houses, chase the enemy into the thresholds, lintels, doors, verandas, pillars, and so on, again not letting him see his situation.

Always chase the enemy into bad footholds, obstacles at the side, and so on, using the virtues of the place to establish predominant positions from which to fight. You must research and train diligently in this.

大石主税藤原良金

無禄　部屋住

良雄の嫡男ふして母ハ但州
豊岡の藩石束源五
兵衛の女すり良金
十四才ふて國難ふあひ
父の命に志るつて優
讐言の列ふ入り翌年
九月小野寺と共ふ武州川嵜よて
元服し討入の時ハ
搦手の首長として
まいろ込働をうふり
死たる時十六才辭世

　極樂の
　　をいひと助君ころに
　ひ孫胞をそへて四十八人

刃上樹劔信士

三つの先と云事

三つの先、一つハ我方より敵へかゝる先、
けんの先といふ也。又一つハ、
敵より我方へかゝる時の先、
是ハたいの先と云也。
又一つハ、我もかゝり、敵も
かゝりあふときの先、躰々の先と云。
これ三つの先也。
何の戦初にも、此三つの先より外ハなし。
先の次第をもつて、はや勝事を得ものなれバ、
先と云事、兵法の第一也。
此先の子細、さま／＼有といへども、
其時々の理を先とし、敵の心を見、
我兵法の智恵をもつて勝事なれバ、
こまやかに書分る事にあらず。

The three methods to forestall the enemy[32]

The first is to forestall him by attacking. This is called *Ken No Sen* (to set him up).

Another method is to forestall him as he attacks. This is called *Tai No Sen* (to wait for the initiative).

The other method is when you and the enemy attack together. This is called *Tai Tai No Sen* (to accompany him and forestall him).

There are no methods of taking the lead other than these three. Because you can win quickly by taking the lead, it is one of the most important things in strategy. There are several things involved in taking the lead. You must make the best of the situation, see through the enemy's spirit so that you grasp his strategy and defeat him. It is impossible to write about this in detail.

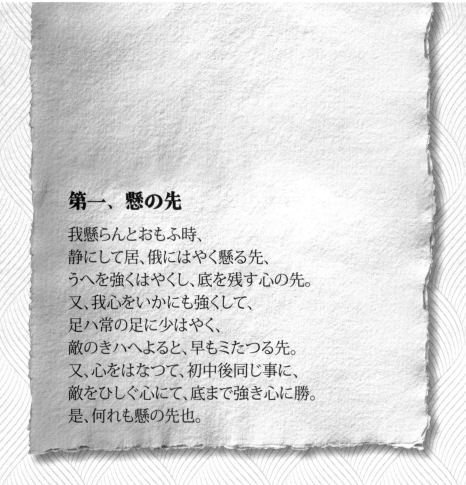

第一、懸の先

我懸らんとおもふ時、
静にして居、俄にはやく懸る先、
うへを強くはやくし、底を残す心の先。
又、我心をいかにも強くして、
足ハ常の足に少はやく、
敵のきハへよると、早もミたつる先。
又、心をはなつて、初中後同じ事に、
敵をひしぐ心にて、底まで強き心に勝。
是、何れも懸の先也。

The first – Ken No Sen

When you decide to attack, keep calm and dash in quickly, forestalling the enemy. Or you can advance seemingly strongly but with a reserved spirit, forestalling him with the reserve.

Alternatively, advance with as strong a spirit as possible, and when you reach the enemy move with your feet a little quicker than normal, unsettling him and overwhelming him sharply.

Or, with your spirit calm, attack with a feeling of constantly crushing the enemy, from first to last. The spirit is to win in the depths of the enemy.

These are all Ken No Sen.

第二、待の先

敵我方へかゝりくる時、
少もかまはず、よはきやうにミせて、
敵ちかくなつて、づんと強くはなれて、
とびつくやうにミせて、敵のたるミを見て、
直に強く勝事。これ一つの先。
又、敵かゝりくるとき、
我もなを強くなつて出るとき、
敵のかゝる拍子の替る間をうけ、
其まゝ勝を得事。是、待の先の理也。

The second – Tai No Sen

When the enemy attacks, remain undisturbed but feign weakness. As the enemy reaches
you, suddenly move away indicating that you intend to jump aside, then dash in attacking
strongly as soon as you see the enemy relax. This is one way.

Or, as the enemy attacks, attack more strongly, taking advantage of the resulting
disorder in his timing to win.

This is the Tai No Sen principle.

第三、躰々の先

敵はやく懸るにハ、
我静につよくかゝり、敵ちかくなつて、
づんとおもひきる身にして、
敵のゆとりのミゆる時、直に強く勝。
又、敵静にかゝるとき、
我身うきやかに、少はやくかゝりて、
敵近くなつて、ひともミもみ、
敵の色にしたがひ、強く勝事。
是、躰々の先也。
此儀、こまかに書分けがたし。
此書付をもつて、大かた工夫有べし。
此三つの先、時にしたがひ、理にしたがひ、
いつにても我方よりかゝる事にハ
あらざるものなれども、
同じくハ、我方よりかゝりて、
敵を自由にまはしたき事也。
何れも先の事、兵法の智力をもつて、
必勝事を得る心、能々鍛錬有べし。

The third – Tai Tai No Sen

When the enemy makes a quick attack, you must attack strongly and calmly, aim for his weak point as he draws near, and strongly defeat him.

Or, if the enemy attacks calmly, you must observe his movement and, with your body rather floating, join in with his movements as he draws near. Move quickly and cut him strongly.

This is Tai Tai No Sen.

These things cannot be clearly explained in words. You must research what is written here. In these three ways of forestalling, you must judge the situation. This does not mean that you always attack first; but if the enemy attacks first you can lead him around. In strategy, you have effectively won when you forestall the enemy, so you must train well to attain this.

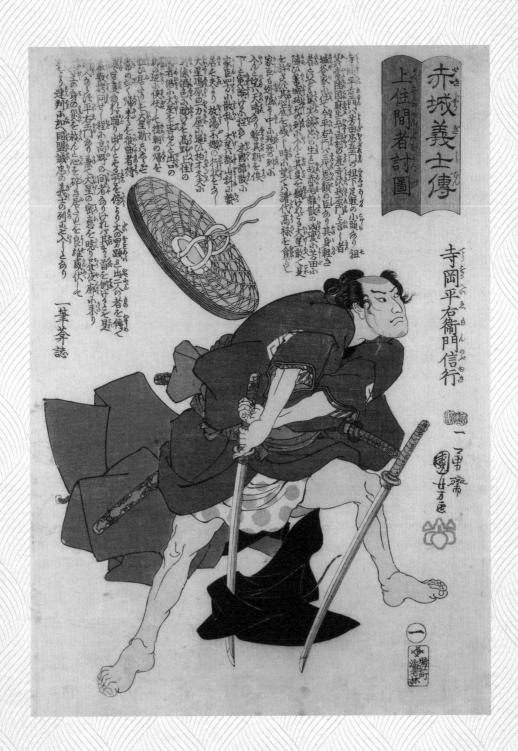

枕を押ると云事

枕をおさゆるとハ、
かしらをあげさせずと云所也。
兵法勝負の道にかぎつて、
人に我身をまはされて、あとにつく事、悪し。
いかにもして、敵を自由にまはしたき事也。
然によつて、敵も左様に思ひ、
われも其心あれども、人のする事を
うけがはずしてハ、叶がたし。
兵法に、人のうつ所をとめ、つく所をおさへ、
くむ所をもぎはなしなどする事也。
枕を押ると云ハ、我実の道を得て、
敵にかゝりあふ時、敵何事にても思ふ
氣ざしを、敵のせぬうちに見しりて、
敵の打と云、うの字のかしらをおさへて、
跡をさせざる心、是枕をおさゆる心也。
たとへバ、敵の懸ると云、かの字（のかしら）を
おさへ、飛と云、との字のかしらをおさへ、
きると云、きの字のかしらをおさゆる事、
ミなもつておなじ心也。
敵我にわざをなす事につけて、
役にたゝざる事をば敵に任せ、
役に立ほどの事をバ、おさへて、
敵にさせぬやうにする所、兵法の専也。
これも、敵のする事をおさへん／＼とする心、
後手也。先、我は何事にても、
道にまかせてわざをなすうちに、
敵もわざをせんと思ふかしらをおさへて、
何事も役にたゝせず、敵をこなす所、
是、兵法の達者、鍛錬の故也。
枕をおさゆる事、能々吟味有べき也。

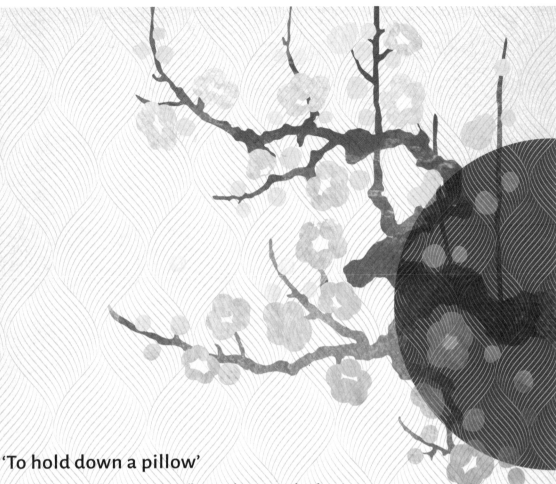

'To hold down a pillow'

'To hold down a pillow' means not allowing the enemy's head to rise.

In contests of strategy, it is bad to be led about by the enemy. You must always be able to lead the enemy about. Obviously, the enemy will also be thinking of doing this, but he cannot forestall you if you do not allow him to come out. In strategy, you must stop the enemy as he attempts to cut; you must push down his thrust, and throw off his hold when he tries to grapple. This is the meaning of 'to hold down a pillow'. When you have grasped this principle, whatever the enemy tries to bring about in the fight you will see in advance and suppress it. The spirit is to check his attack at the syllable 'at . . .'; when he jumps, check his advance at the syllable 'ju . . .'; and check his cut at 'cu . . .'.

The important thing in strategy is to suppress the enemy's useful actions but allow his useless actions. However, doing this alone is defensive. First, you must act according to the Way, suppress the enemy's techniques, foil his plans, and thence command him directly. When you can do this, you will be a master of strategy. You must train well and research 'holding down a pillow'.

とをこすと云事

渡をこすと云ハ、縦ば海をわたるに、
せとゝいふ所も有、又は、四十里五十里とも
長き海をこす所を、渡と云。
人間の世をわたるにも、一代のうちにハ、
渡をこすと云所多かるべし。
舩路にして、其との所を知り、
舟の位をしり、日なミを能知りて、
たとひ友舩は出さずとも、
その時のくらゐをうけ、
或はひらきの風にたより、或は追風をもうけ、
若、風かはりても、二里三里は、
ろかひをもつて湊に着と心得て、
舩をのりとり、渡を越す所也。
其心を得て、人の世を渡るにも、
一大事にかけて、渡をこすと思ふ心有べし。
兵法、戦のうちに、渡をこす事肝要也。
敵の位をうけ、我身の達者をおぼへ、
其理をもつてとをこす事、
よき船頭の海路を越すと同じ。
渡を越てハ、又心安き所也。
渡を越といふ事、敵によはミをつけ、
我身先になりて、大かたはや勝所也。
大小の兵法のうへにも、とをこすと云心、肝要也。
能々吟味有べし。

'Crossing at a ford'

'Crossing at a ford' means, for example, crossing the sea at a strait, or crossing over a hundred miles of broad sea at a crossing place. I believe this 'crossing at a ford' occurs often in a man's lifetime. It means setting sail even though your friends stay in harbour, knowing the route, knowing the soundness of your ship and the favour of the day. When all the conditions are met, and there is perhaps a favourable wind, or a tailwind, then set sail. If the wind changes within a few miles of your destination, you must row across the remaining distance without sail.

If you attain this spirit, it applies to everyday life. You must always think of crossing at a ford.

In strategy, also, it is important to 'cross at a ford'. Discern the enemy's capability and, knowing your own strong points, 'cross the ford' at the advantageous place, as a good captain crosses a sea route. If you succeed in crossing at the best place, you may take your ease. To cross at a ford means to attack the enemy's weak point, and to put yourself in an advantageous position. This is how to win in large-scale strategy. The spirit of crossing at a ford is necessary in both large- and small-scale strategy.

You must research this well.

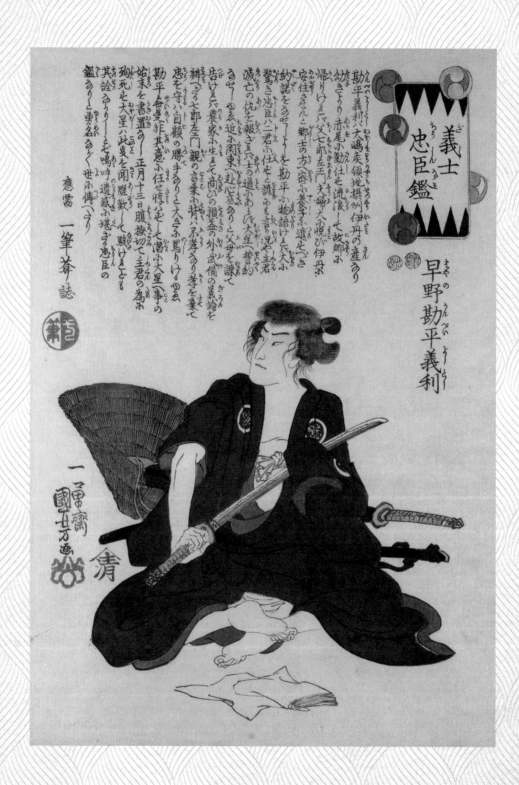

THE BOOK OF FIVE RINGS

けいきを知と云事

景氣をみると云ハ、大分の兵法にしてハ、
敵のさかへ、おとろへを知り、
相手の人数の心を知り、其場の位をうけ、
敵のけいきを能見分、我人数何としかけ、
此兵法の理にてたしかに勝と云ところを
のミ込て、先の位をしつて戦所也。
又、一分の兵法も、敵のながれをわきまへ、
相手の強弱、人がらを見分け、
敵の氣色にちがふ事をしかけ、
敵のめりかりを知り、其間の拍子をよく知て、
先をしかくる所、肝要也。
物毎のけいきといふ事ハ、
我智力強けれバ、かならずミゆる所也。
兵法自由の身になりてハ、
敵の心を能斗て勝道多かるべき事也。
工夫有べし。

'To know the times'

'To know the times' means to know the enemy's disposition in battle. Is it flourishing or waning? By observing the spirit of the enemy's men and getting the best position, you can work out the enemy's disposition and move your men accordingly. You can win through this principle of strategy, fighting from a position of advantage.

When in a duel, you must forestall the enemy and attack when you have first recognized his school of strategy, perceived his quality and his strong and weak points. Attack in an unsuspected manner, knowing his metre and modulation and the appropriate timing.

Knowing the times means, if your ability is high, seeing right into things. If you are thoroughly conversant with strategy, you will recognize the enemy's intentions and thus have many opportunities to win. You must sufficiently study this.

けんをふむと云事

劔を踏と云心ハ、兵法に専用る儀也。
先、大なる兵法にしてハ、
弓鉄炮におゐても、敵、我方へうちかけ、
何事にてもしかくる時、
敵の弓鉄炮にてもはなしかけて、
其跡にかゝるによつて、又矢をつがひ、
鉄炮にくすりをこみ合するによつて、
又新しくなつて追込がたし。
弓鉄炮にても、
敵のはなつ内に、はやかゝる心也。
はやくかゝれバ、矢もつがひがたし、
鉄炮もうち得ざる心也。
物ごとに敵のしかくると、
其まゝ其理をうけて、
敵のする事を踏付てかつこゝろ也。
又、一分の兵法も、
敵の打出す太刀の跡へうてバ、
とたん／＼となりて、はかゆかざる所也。
敵のうち出す太刀ハ、
足にて踏付る心にして、打出す所を勝、
二度目を敵の打得ざる様にすべし。
踏と云ハ、足には限るべからず。
身にてもふミ、心にても蹈、
勿論太刀にてもふミ付て、
二の目を敵によくさせざる様に心得べし。
是則、物毎の先の心也。
敵と一度にと云て、ゆきあたる心にてハなし。
其まゝ跡に付心也。能々吟味有べし。

'To tread down the sword'

'To tread down the sword' is a principle often used in strategy. First, in large-scale strategy, when the enemy first discharges bows and guns and then attacks, it is difficult for us to attack if we are busy loading powder into our guns or notching our arrows. The spirit is to attack quickly while the enemy is still shooting with bows or guns. The spirit is to win by 'treading down' as we receive the enemy's attack.

In single combat, we cannot get a decisive victory by cutting, with a 'tee-dum, tee-dum' feeling, in the wake of the enemy's attacking long sword. We must defeat him at the start of his attack, in the spirit of treading him down with the feet, so that he cannot rise again to the attack.

'Treading' does not simply mean treading with the feet. Tread with the body, tread with the spirit, and, of course, tread and cut with the long sword. You must achieve the spirit of not allowing the enemy to attack a second time. This is the spirit of forestalling in every sense. Once at the enemy, you should not aspire just to strike him, but to cling after the attack. You must study this deeply.

くづれを知と云事

崩と云事ハ、物毎に有もの物也。
其家の崩るゝ、身のくづるゝ、
敵の崩るゝ事も、時にあたりて、
拍子ちがひになつて、くづるゝ所也。
大分の兵法にしても、
敵の崩るゝ拍子を得て、
其間をぬかさぬやうに追立る事、肝要也。
くづるゝ所のいきをぬかしてハ、
たてかへす所有べし。
又、一分の兵法にも、戦ふ内に、
敵の拍子ちがひて、くづれめのつくもの也。
其ほどを油断すれば、又立かへり、
新しくなりて、はかゆかざる所也。
其くづれめにつき、敵のかほたてなをさゞる様に、
たしかに追かくる所、肝要也。
追かくるハ、直に強きこゝろ也。
敵立かへさゞるやうに、打はなすもの也
うちはなすと云事、能々分別有べし。

To know 'collapse'

Everything can collapse. Houses, bodies, and enemies collapse when their rhythm becomes deranged.

In large-scale strategy, when the enemy starts to collapse, you must pursue him without letting the chance go. If you fail to take advantage of your enemies' collapse, they may recover.

In single combat, the enemy sometimes loses timing and collapses. If you let this opportunity pass, he may recover and not be so negligent thereafter. Fix your eye on the enemy's collapse, and chase him, attacking so that you do not let him recover. You must do this. The chasing attack is with a strong spirit. You must utterly cut the enemy down so that he does not recover his position. You must understand utterly how to cut down the enemy.

敵になると云事

敵になると云ハ、我身を
敵になり替りておもふべきと云所也。
世の中を見るに、ぬすミなどして、
家のうちへとり籠るやうなるものをも、
敵を強くおもひなすもの也。
敵になりておもへバ、
世の中の人をみな相手として、
にげこミて、せんかたなき心也。
とりこもる者ハ雉子也、打はたしに入人ハ鷹也。
能々工夫有べし。
大なる兵法にしても、敵といへバ、
強くおもひて、大事にかくるもの也。
我常によき人数を持、兵法の道理を能知り、
敵に勝と云所を能うけてハ、
氣づかひすべき道にあらず。
一分の兵法も、敵になりて思ふべし。
兵法能心得て、道理強く、其道達者なる者に
あひてハ、かならず負ると思ふ所也。
能々吟味すべし。

'To become the enemy'

'To become the enemy' means to think yourself into the enemy's position. In the world, people tend to think of a robber trapped in a house as a fortified enemy. However, if we think of 'becoming the enemy', we feel that the whole world is against us and that there is no escape. He who is shut inside is a pheasant. He who enters to arrest is a hawk. You must appreciate this.

In large-scale strategy, people are always under the impression that the enemy is strong, and so tend to become cautious. But if you have good soldiers, and if you understand the principles of strategy, and if you know how to beat the enemy, there is nothing to worry about.

In single combat, also, you must put yourself in the enemy's position. If you think, 'Here is a master of the Way, who knows the principles of strategy', then you will surely lose. You must consider this deeply.

四手をはなすと云事

四手をはなすとハ、敵も我も、同じこゝろに、
はりあふ心になつては、
戦はかゆかざるもの也。
はりあふ心になるとおもハゞ、其まゝ心を捨て、
別の利にて勝事をしる也。
大分の兵法にしても、
四手の心にあれば、はかゆかず、
人も多く損ずる事也。はやく心を捨て、
敵のおもはざる利にて勝事、専也。
又、一分の兵法にても、
四手になるとおもハゞ、其まゝ心をかへて、
敵の位を得て、各別かはりたる利を以て
勝をわきまゆる事、肝要也。
能々分別すべし。

'To release four hands'

'To release four hands'[33] is used when you and the enemy are contending with the same spirit, and the issue cannot be decided. Abandon this spirit and win through an alternative resource.

In large-scale strategy, when there is a 'four hands' spirit, do not give up – it is man's existence. Immediately throw away this spirit and win with a technique the enemy does not expect.

In single combat also, when we think we have fallen into the 'four hands' situation, we must defeat the enemy by changing our mind and applying a suitable technique according to his condition. You must be able to judge this.

かげをうごかすと云事

かげをうごかすと云ハ、
敵の心のミへわかぬ時の事也。
大分の兵法にしても、
何とも敵の位の見わけざる時ハ、
我方より強くしかくる様にみせて、
敵の手だてを見るもの也。手だてを見てハ、
各別の利にて勝事、やすき所也。
又、一分の兵法にしても、
敵うしろに太刀を構、脇に構たる様なるときハ、
ふつとうたんとすれバ、
敵思ふ心を太刀にあらはすもの也。
あらはれしるゝにおゐてハ、其まゝ利をうけて、
たしかにかちをしるべきもの也。
油断すれバ、拍子ぬくるもの也。
能々吟味有べし。

影をおさゆると云事

かげを押ると云ハ、敵のかたより、
しかくる心の見へたるときの事也。
大分の兵法にしてハ、
敵のわざをせんとする所を、おさゆると云て、
我方より其利を押る所を、敵に強く見すれば、
強きにおされて、敵の心かはる事也。
我も心をちがへて、空なる心より、
先をしかけて勝所也。
一分の兵法にしても、
敵のおこる強き氣ざしを、
利の拍子を以てやめさせ、
やみたる拍子に、我勝利をうけて、
先をしかくるもの也。能々工夫有べし。

'To move the shadow'

'To move the shadow' is used when you cannot see the enemy's spirit.

In large-scale strategy, when you cannot see the enemy's position, indicate that you are about to attack strongly, to discover his resources. It is easy then to defeat him with a different method once you see his resources.

In single combat, if the enemy takes up a rear or side attitude of the long sword so that you cannot see his intention, make a feint attack, and the enemy will show his long sword, thinking he sees your spirit. Benefiting from what you are shown, you can win with certainty. If you are negligent, you will miss the timing. Research this well.

'To hold down a shadow'

'Holding down a shadow' is used when you can see the enemy's attacking spirit.

In large-scale strategy, when the enemy embarks on an attack, if you make a show of strongly suppressing his technique, he will change his mind. Then, altering your spirit, defeat him by forestalling him with a Void spirit.

Or, in single combat, hold down the enemy's strong intention with a suitable timing, and defeat him by forestalling him with this timing. You must study this well.

忠臣藏夜討之取之圖

うつらかすと云事

うつらかすと云ハ、物ごとに有るもの也。
或ハねむりなどもうつり、或ハあくびなども
うつるもの也。時の移もあり。
大分の兵法にして、
敵うはきにして、ことをいそぐ心のミゆる時は、
少もそれにかまはざるやうにして、
いかにもゆるりとなりて見すれバ、
敵も我事にうけて、きざしたるむもの也。
其うつりたると思とき、
我方より、空の心にして、
はやく強くしかけて、勝利を得るもの也。
一分の兵法にしても、
我身も心もゆるりとして、敵のたるみの間をうけて、
強くはやく先にしかけて勝所、専也。
又、よハすると云て、是に似たる事有。
一つハ、たいくつの心、一つハ、うかつく心、
一つハ、弱くなる心。能々工夫有べし。

むかづかすると云事

むかづかすると云ハ、物毎にあり。
一つにハ、きはどき心、
二つにハ、むりなる心。
三つにハ、思はざる心。能吟味有べし。
大分の兵法にして、
むかづかする事、肝要也。
敵のおもはざる所へ、いきどふしくしかけて、
敵の心のきはまらざるうちに、
わが利を以て、先をしかけて勝事、肝要也。

又、一分の兵法にしても、
初ゆるりと見せて、俄に強くかゝり、
敵の心のめりかり、はたらきにしたがひ、
いきをぬかさず、其まゝ利をうけて、
かちをわきまゆる事、肝要也。
能々吟味有べし。

To pass on

Many things are said to be passed on. Sleepiness can be passed on, and yawning can be passed on. Time can be passed on also.

In large-scale strategy, when the enemy is agitated and shows an inclination to rush, do not mind in the least. Make a show of complete calmness, and the enemy will be taken by this and will become relaxed. When you see that this spirit has been passed on, you can bring about the enemy's defeat by attacking strongly with a Void spirit.

In single combat, you can win by relaxing your body and spirit and then, catching on the moment the enemy relaxes, attack strongly and quickly, forestalling him.

What is known as 'getting someone drunk' is similar to this. You can also infect the enemy with a bored, careless, or weak spirit. You must study this well.

To cause loss of balance

Many things can cause a loss of balance. One cause is danger, another is hardship, and another is surprise. You must research this.

In large-scale strategy, it is important to cause loss of balance. Attack without warning where the enemy is not expecting it, and while his spirit is undecided follow up your advantage and, having the lead, defeat him.

Or, in single combat, start by making a show of being slow, then suddenly attack strongly. Without allowing him space for breath to recover from the fluctuation of spirit, you must grasp the opportunity to win. Get the feel of this.

おびやかすと云事

おびゆると云ハ、物毎に有事也。
思ひもよらぬ事におびゆる心也。
大分の兵法にしても、敵をおびやかす事、肝要也。
或ハ、ものゝ聲にてもおびやかし、
或ハ、小を大にしておびやかし、
又、片脇よりふつとおびやかす事。
是おびゆる所也。
其おびゆる拍子を得て、其利を以て勝べし。
一分の兵法にしても、身を以ておびやかし、
太刀を以ておびやかし、声を以ておびやかし、
敵の心になき事、ふつとしかけて、
おびゆる所の利をうけて、其まゝ勝を得事、肝要也。
能々吟味有べし。

まぶるゝと云事

まぶるゝと云ハ、敵我ちかくなつて、
たがひに強くはり合て、
はかゆかざるとミれバ、
其まゝ敵とひとつにまぶれあひて、
まぶれ合たる其内の利を以て勝事、肝要也。
大分小分の兵法にも、
敵我かたわけてハ、たがひに
心はりあひて、勝のつかざるときハ、
其まゝ敵にまぶれて、
たがひにわけなくなるやうにして、
其内の徳を得て、其内の勝をしりて、
強く勝事、専也。能々吟味有べし。

To frighten

Fright often occurs, caused by the unexpected.

In large-scale strategy, you can frighten the enemy not by what you present to their eyes, but by shouting, making a small force seem large, or by threatening them from the flank without warning. These things all frighten. You can win by making best use of the enemy's frightened rhythm.

In single combat, also, you must use the advantage of taking the enemy unawares by frightening him with your body, long sword, or voice, to defeat him. You should research this well.

'To soak in'

When you have come to grips, and are striving together with the enemy, and you realize that you cannot advance, you 'soak in' and become one with the enemy. You can win by applying a suitable technique while you are mutually entangled.

In battles involving large numbers as well as in fights with small numbers, you can often win decisively with the advantage of knowing how to 'soak' into the enemy, whereas, were you to draw apart, you would lose the chance to win. Research this well.

かどにさはると云事

角にさはると云ハ、ものごと、強き物をおすに、
其まゝ直にはおしこミがたきもの也。
大分の兵法にしても、
敵の人数を見て、はり出強き所のかどに
あたりて、其利を得べし。
かどのめるに随ひ、惣もミなめる心あり。
其める内にも、かど／＼に心を付て、
勝利を得事、肝要也。
一分の兵法にしても、
敵の躰のかどにいたミを付、
其躰少も弱くなり、くづるゝ躰になりてハ、
勝事安きもの也。此事能々吟味して、
勝所をわきまゆる事、専也。

うろめかすと云事

うろめかすと云ハ、敵にたしかなる心を
もたせざるやうにする所也。
大分の兵法にしても、
戦の場におゐて、敵の心をはかり、
我兵法の智力を以て、敵の心をそこ爰となし、
とのかうのと思はせ、おそしはやしと思はせ、
敵のうろめく心になる拍子を得て、
たしかに勝所をわきまゆる事也。
又、一分の兵法にして、
時にあたりて、色々のわざをしかけ、
或ハうつとミせ、或ハつくと見せ、
又ハ入こむと思はせ、敵のうろめく氣ざしを得て、
自由に勝所、是戦の専也。
能々吟味有べし。

'To injure the corners'

It is difficult to move strong things by pushing directly, so you should 'injure the corners'.

In large-scale strategy, it is beneficial to strike at the corners of the enemy's force. If the corners are overthrown, the spirit of the whole body will be overthrown. To defeat the enemy, you must follow up the attack when the corners have fallen.

In single combat, it is easy to win once the enemy collapses. This happens when you injure the 'corners' of his body, and this weakens him. It is important to know how to do this, so you must research it deeply.

To throw into confusion

This means making the enemy lose resolve.

In large-scale strategy, we can use our troops to confuse the enemy on the field. Observing the enemy's spirit, we can make him think, 'Here? There? Like that? Like this? Slow? Fast?' Victory is certain when the enemy is caught up in a rhythm that confuses his spirit.

In single combat, we can confuse the enemy by attacking with varied techniques when the chance arises. Feint a thrust or cut, or make the enemy think you are going close to him, and when he is confused you can easily win.

This is the essence of fighting, and you must research it deeply.

三つの聲と云事

三つのこゑとハ、初中後の聲と云て、
三つにかけわくる事也。
所により、聲をかくると云事、専也。
聲ハ、いきおひなるによつて、火事などにもかけ、
風波にも聲をかけ、勢力をミする也。
大分の兵法にしても、
戦よりはじめにかくる聲ハ、
いかほどもかさを懸て聲をかけ、
又、戦間のこゑハ、調子をひきく、
底より出る聲にてかゝり、
かちて後に大きに強くかくる聲、
是三つの聲也。
又、一分の兵法にしても、
敵をうごかさんため、打と見せて、
かしらより、ゑいと聲をかけ、
聲の跡より太刀を打出すもの也。
又、敵を打てあとに聲をかくる事、勝をしらする聲也。
これを先後のこゑと云。
太刀と一度に大きに聲をかくる事なし。
若、戦の中にかくるハ、
拍子に乗る聲、ひきくかくる也。
能々吟味有べし。

横川勘平藤原宗則

徒頭
禄　廿五両五人扶持

The Three Shouts

The Three Shouts are divided thus: before, during and after. Shout according to the situation. The voice is a thing of life. We shout against fires and so on, against the wind and the waves. The voice shows energy.

In large-scale strategy, at the start of battle we shout as loudly as possible. During the fight, the voice is low-pitched, shouting out as we attack. After the contest, we shout in the wake of our victory. These are the Three Shouts.

In single combat, we make as if to cut and shout 'Ei!' at the same time to disturb the enemy, then in the wake of our shout we cut with the long sword. We shout after we have cut down the enemy – this is to announce victory. This is called 'sen go no koe' (before and after voice). We do not shout simultaneously with flourishing the long sword. We shout during the fight to get into rhythm. Research this deeply.

まぎると云事

まぎると云ハ、大分の戦にしてハ、
人数をたがひに立合、敵の強きとき、
まぎると云て、敵の一方へかゝり、
敵くづるゝとミバ、すてゝ、
又強き方々へかゝる。
大方、つゞら折にかゝる心也。
一分の兵法にして、
敵を大勢よするも、此心専也。
方々へかゝり、方々にげバ、
又強き方へかゝり、敵の拍子を得て、
よき拍子に、左、右と、
つゞら折の心に思ひて、
敵のいろを見合て、かゝるもの也。
其敵の位を得、打通るにおゐてハ、
少も引心なく、強く勝利也。
一分入身のときも、
敵の強きには、其心あり。
まぎると云事、一足も引事をしらず、
まぎりゆくと云心、能々分別すべし。

To mingle

In battles, when the armies are in confrontation, attack the enemy's strong points and, when you see that they are beaten back, quickly separate and attack yet another strong point on the periphery of his force. The spirit of this is like a winding mountain path.

This is an important fighting method for one man against many. Strike down the enemies in one quarter, or drive them back, then grasp the timing and attack further strong points to right and left, as if on a winding mountain path, weighing up the enemies' disposition. When you know the enemies' level, attack strongly with no trace of retreating spirit.

In single combat, too, use this spirit with the enemy's strong points.

What is meant by 'mingling' is the spirit of advancing and becoming engaged with the enemy, and not withdrawing even one step. You must understand this.

ひしぐと云事

ひしぐと云ハ、たとヘバ、
敵を弱くみなして、我つよめになつて、
ひしぐと云心、専也。
大分の兵法にしても、
敵小人数の位を見こなし、又は、
大勢なりとも、敵うろめきて、
よはミ付所なれバ、ひしぐと云て、
かしらよりかさをかけて、おつひしぐ心也。
ひしぐ事弱ければ、もてかへす事有。
手のうちににぎつてひしぐ心、
能々分別すべし。
又、一分の兵法の時も、
我手に不足のもの、又は、
敵の拍子ちがひ、すさりめになる時、
少もいきをくれず、めを見合ざる様になし、
真直にひしぎつくる事、肝要也。
少もおきたてさせぬ所、第一也。
能々吟味有べし。

To crush

This means to crush the enemy, regarding him as being weak.

In large-scale strategy, when we see that the enemy has few men, or if he has many men but his spirit is weak and disordered, we knock the hat over his eyes, crushing him utterly. If we crush lightly, he may recover. You must learn the spirit of crushing as if with a hand-grip.

In single combat, if the enemy is less skilful than yourself, if his rhythm is disorganized, or if he has fallen into evasive or retreating attitudes, we must crush him straightaway, with no concern for his presence and without allowing him space for breath. It is essential to crush him all at once. The primary thing is not to let him recover his position even a little. You must research this deeply.

さんかいのかはりと云事

山海のかはりと云ハ、敵我戦のうちに、
同じ事を度々する事、悪敷所也。
同じ事、二度ハ是非に及ばず、
三度とするにあらず。
敵にわざをしかくるに、
一度にてもちゐずバ、今一つも
せきかけて、其利に及ばずバ、
各別かはりたる事を、ぼつとしかけ、
夫にもはかゆかずバ、
又各別の事をしかくべし。
然によつて、敵、山とおもはゞ、海としかけ、
海と思はゞ、山としかくる心、兵法の道也。
能々吟味有べき事也。

The 'mountain-sea change'

The 'mountain-sea' spirit means that it is bad to repeat the same thing several times when fighting the enemy. There may be no help but to do something twice, but do not try it a third time. If you once make an attack and fail, there is little chance of success if you use the same approach again. If you attempt a technique which you have previously tried unsuccessfully and fail yet again, then you must change your attacking method.

If the enemy thinks of the mountains, attack like the sea; and if he thinks of the sea, attack like the mountains. You must research this deeply.

そこをぬくと云事

底を抜と云ハ、敵と戦に、
其道の利をもつて、上ハ勝と見ゆれども、
心をたへさゞるによつて、
上にてはまけ、下の心はまけぬ事有。
其儀におゐては、
我俄に替りたる心になつて、
敵の心をたやし、底よりまくる心に
敵のなる所、みる事専也。
此底をぬく事、太刀にてもぬき、
又、身にてもぬき、心にてもぬく所あり。
一道にハ、わきまふべからず。
底よりくづれたるハ、我心残すに及ばず。
さなき時は、残(す)心也。
残す心あれば、敵くづれがたき事也。
大分小分の兵法にしても、
底をぬく所、能々鍛練有べし。

あらたになると云事

新に成と云ハ、敵我もつるゝ心になつて、
はかゆかざる時、我氣をふり捨て、
物毎を新しくはじむる心に思ひて、
其拍子をうけて、かちをわきまゆる所也。

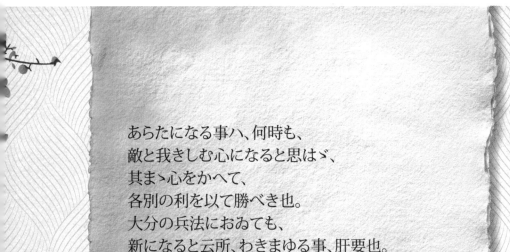

あらたになる事ハ、何時も、
敵と我きしむ心になると思はゞ、
其まゝ心をかへて、
各別の利を以て勝べき也。
大分の兵法におゐても、
新になると云所、わきまゆる事、肝要也。
能々吟味有べし。

'To penetrate the depths'

When we are fighting with the enemy, even when it can be seen that we can win on the surface with the benefit of the Way, if his spirit is not extinguished, he may be beaten superficially yet undefeated in spirit deep inside. With this principle of 'penetrating the depths' we can destroy the enemy's spirit in its depths, demoralizing him by quickly changing our spirit. This often occurs.

Penetrating the depths means penetrating with the long sword, penetrating with the body, and penetrating with the spirit. This cannot be understood in a generalization.

Once we have crushed the enemy in the depths, there is no need to remain spirited. But otherwise we must remain spirited. If the enemy remains spirited, it is difficult to crush him. You must train in penetrating the depths for large-scale strategy and also single combat.

'To renew'

'To renew' applies when we are fighting with the enemy, and an entangled spirit arises where there is no possible resolution. We must abandon our efforts, think of the situation in a fresh spirit, then win in the new rhythm. To renew, when we are deadlocked with the enemy, means that without changing our circumstance we change our spirit and win through a different technique.

It is necessary to consider how 'to renew' also applies in large-scale strategy. Research this diligently.

そとうごしゆと云事

鼠頭午首と云ハ、敵と戦のうちに、
たがひにこまかなる所を思ひ合て、
もつるゝ心になる時、
兵法の道を、常に鼠頭午首／＼とおもひて、
いかにもこまかなるうちに、
俄に大きなる心にして、
大、小に替る事、兵法一つの心だて也。
平生、人の心も、そとふごしゆと思べき所、
武士の肝心也。
兵法、大分小分にしても、此心、はなるべからず。
此事、能々吟味有べきもの也。

しやうそつをしると云事

将卒を知るとハ、何も戦に及とき、
我思ふ道に至てハ、たへず此法をおこなひ、
兵法の智力を得て、わが敵たるものをバ、
ミなわが卒なりと思ひとつて、
なしたきやうになすべしと心得、
敵を自由にまはさんと思ふ所、
われハ将也、敵ハ卒也。
工夫有べし。

'Rat's head, ox's neck'

'Rat's head, ox's neck' means that, when we are fighting with the enemy and both he and we have become occupied with small points in an entangled spirit, we must always think of the Way of strategy as being both a rat's head and an ox's neck. Whenever we have become preoccupied with small details, we must suddenly change into a large spirit, interchanging large with small.

This is one of the essences of strategy. It is necessary that the warrior think in this spirit in everyday life. You must not depart from this spirit in large-scale strategy nor in single combat.

'The commander knows the troops'

'The commander knows the troops' applies everywhere in fights in my Way of strategy.

Using the wisdom of strategy, think of the enemy as your own troops. When you think in this way, you can move him at will and be able to chase him around. You become the general and the enemy becomes your troops. You must master this.

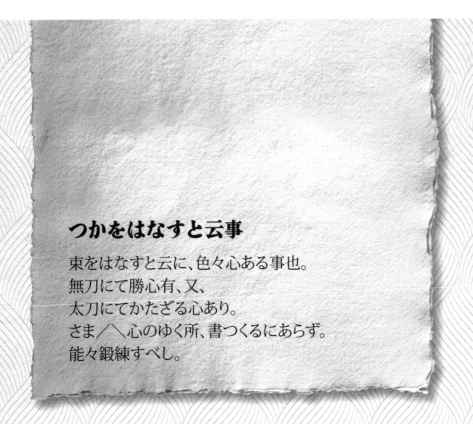

つかをはなすと云事

束をはなすと云に、色々心ある事也。
無刀にて勝心有、又、
太刀にてかたざる心あり。
さま／〝心のゆく所、書つくるにあらず。
能々鍛練すべし。

'To let go the hilt'

There are various kinds of spirit involved in letting go the hilt.

There is the spirit of winning without a sword. There is also the spirit of holding the long sword but not winning. The various methods cannot be expressed in writing. You must train well.

いはをの身と云事

巖の身と云ハ、兵法を得道して、
忽巖のごとくになつて、
萬事あたらざる所、うごかざる所。（口傳）
右、書付る所、一流劍術の場にして、
たへず思ひよる事のミ、書顯し置もの也。
今始て此利を記すものなれバ、
跡先と書紛るゝ心ありて、
こまやかにハ、いひわけがたし。
さりながら、此道をまなぶべき人のためにハ、
心しるしになるべきもの也。
我若年より以來、兵法の道に心をかけ、
劍術一通りの事にも、手をからし、身をからし、
いろ／＼さま／＼の心になり、
他の流々をも尋みるに、
或ハ口にていひかこつけ、
或ハ手にてこまかなるわざをし、
人めによき様にみすると云ても、
一つも實の心にあるべからず。
勿論、かやうの事しならひても、
身をきかせならひ、心をきかせつくる事と
思へども、皆是道のやまひとなりて、
のち／＼迄もうせがたくして、
兵法の直道、世にくち、道のすたるもとゐ也。
劍術、實の道になつて、敵と戰勝事、
此法聊かはる事有べからず。
我兵法の智力を得て、
直なる所を行ふにおゐてハ、
勝事うたがひ有べからざるもの也。

The 'body of a rock'[34]

When you have mastered the Way of strategy, you can suddenly make your body like a rock, and ten thousand things cannot touch you. This is the 'body of a rock'.

Oral tradition: You will not be moved.

What is recorded above is what has been constantly on my mind about Ichi school sword-fencing, written down as it came to me. This is the first time I have written about my technique, and the order of things is a bit confused. It is difficult to express it clearly.

This book is a spiritual guide for the man who wishes to learn the Way.

My heart has been inclined to the Way of strategy from my youth onwards. I have devoted myself to training my hand, tempering my body, and attaining the many spiritual attitudes of sword-fencing. If we watch men of other schools discussing theory, and concentrating on techniques with the hands, even though they seem skilful to watch, they have not the slightest true spirit.

Of course, men who study in this way think they are training the body and spirit, but it is an obstacle to the true Way, and its bad influence remains forever. Thus the true Way of strategy is becoming decadent and dying out.

The true Way of sword-fencing is the craft of defeating the enemy in a fight, and nothing other than this. If you attain and adhere to the wisdom of my strategy, you need never doubt that you will win.

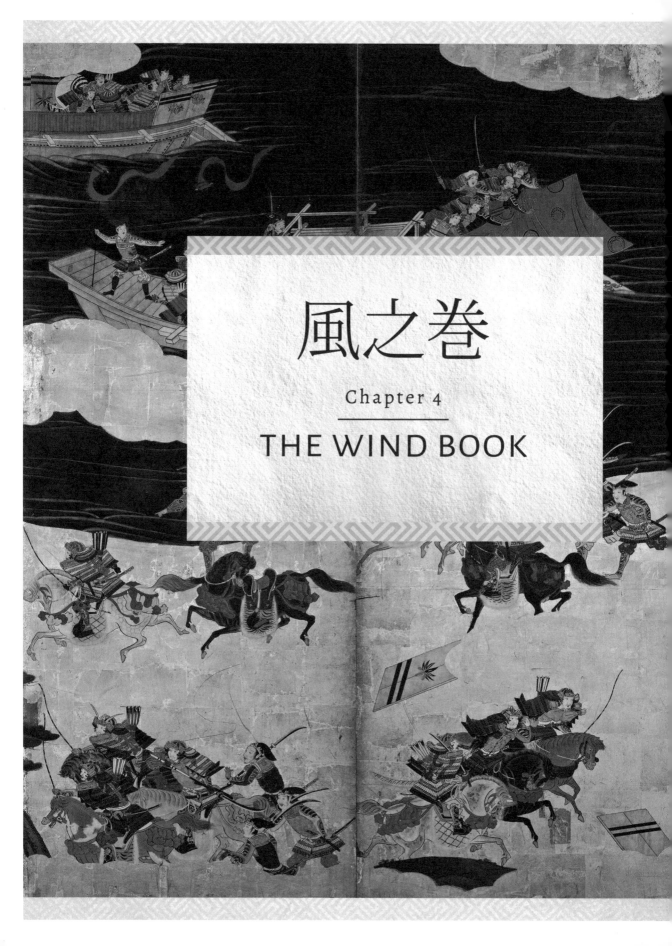

風之巻

Chapter 4

THE WIND BOOK

兵法、他流の道を知る事。
他の兵法の流々を書付、
風之巻として、此巻に顕す所也。
他流の道をしらずしてハ、
一流の道、慥にわきまへがたし。
他の兵法を尋見るに、
大きなる太刀をとつて、強き事を専にして、
其わざをなすながれも有。
或は小太刀といひて、みじかき太刀をもつて、
道を勤むるながれも有。
或ハ、太刀かずおほくたくみ、太刀の構を以て、
表といひ奥として、道を傳ふる流も有。
これミな實の道にあらざる事也。
此巻の奥(内)に慥に書顕し、
善悪利非をしらする也。
我一流の道理、各別の儀也。
他の流々、藝にわたつて身すぎのためにして、
色をかざり、花をさかせ、うり物に
こしらへたるによつて、實の道にあらざる事か。
又、世の中の兵法、劍術ばかりに
ちいさく見立、太刀を振ならひ、
身をきかせて、手のかるゝ所をもつて、
勝事をわきまへたる物か。
いづれもたしかなる道にあらず。
他流の不足なる所、一々此書に書顕す也。
能々吟味して、二刀一流の利を
わきまゆべきもの也。

In strategy, you must know the Ways of other schools, so I have written about various other traditions of strategy in this, the Wind Book.

Without knowledge of the Ways of other schools, it is difficult to understand the essence of my Ichi school. Looking at other schools we find some that specialize in techniques of strength using extra-long swords. Some schools study the Way of the short sword, known as 'kodachi'. Some schools teach dexterity in large numbers of sword techniques, teaching attitudes of the sword as the 'surface' and the Way as the 'interior'.

That none of these are the true Way I show clearly in the interior of this book – all the vices and virtues and rights and wrongs. My Ichi school is different. Other schools make accomplishments their means of livelihood, growing flowers and decoratively colouring articles in order to sell them. This is definitely not the Way of strategy.

Some of the world's strategists are concerned only with sword-fencing, and limit their training to flourishing the long sword and carriage of the body. But is dexterity alone sufficient to win? This is not the essence of the Way.

I have recorded the unsatisfactory points of other schools one by one in this book. You must study these matters deeply to appreciate the benefit of my Nito Ichi school.

他流に大なる太刀をもつ事

他に大なる太刀をこのむ流あり。
我兵法よりして、是を弱き流と見立る也。
其故は、他の兵法、いかさまにも人に勝と云利
をバしらずして、太刀の長きを徳として、
敵相とをき所よりかちたきとおもふに依て、
長き太刀このむ心有べし。
世の中に云、一寸手増りとて、
兵法しらぬものゝ沙汰也。
然に依て、兵法の利なくして、
長きをもつて遠くかたんとする。
夫ハ心のよはき故なるによつて、
よはき兵法と見立る也。
長き太刀このむ身にしてハ、
其いひわけは有ものなれども、
夫ハ其身ひとりの利也。
世の中の實の道より見る時ハ、
道理なき事也。
長き太刀もたずして、みじかき太刀にてハ、
かならずまくべき事か。或ハ其場により、
若、敵相ちかく、組合程の時ハ、
太刀の長きほど、打事もきかず、
太刀もとをりすくなく、太刀をににして、
小わきざし、手ぶりの人に、おとるもの也。
昔より、大ハ小をかなゆるといへば、
むざと長きを嫌ふにはあらず。
長きとかたよる心を嫌ふ儀也。
大分の兵法にして、長太刀ハ大人数也。
みじかきハ小人数也。小人数と大人数と、
合戦ハなるまじきものか。
小人数にて勝こそ、兵法の徳なれ。

むかしも、小人数にて大人数に勝たる例多し。
上下脇などのつまりたる所、
或ハ脇ざしばかりの座にても、太刀をこのむ心、
兵法のうたがひとて、悪敷心也。
人により、少力なる者も有、
其身により、長かたなさす事ならざる身もあり。
我一流におゐて、さやうにかたつきせばき心、
嫌事也。能々吟味有べし。

Other schools using extra-long swords

Some other schools have a liking for extra-long swords. From the point of view of my strategy, these must be seen as weak schools. This is because they do not appreciate the principle of cutting the enemy by any means. Their preference is for the extra-long sword and, relying on the virtue of its length, they think to defeat the enemy from a distance.

In this world it is said, 'One inch gives the hand advantage', but these are the idle words of one who does not know strategy. It shows the inferior strategy of a weak spirit that men should be dependent on the length of their sword, fighting from a distance without the benefit of strategy.

I expect there is a case for the school in question liking extra-long swords as part of its doctrine, but if we compare this with real life it is unreasonable. Surely, we need not necessarily be defeated if we are using a short sword and have no long sword?

It is difficult for these people to cut the enemy when at close quarters because of the length of the long sword. The blade path is large so the long sword is an encumbrance, and they are at a disadvantage compared to the man armed with a short companion sword.

From olden times it has been said: 'Great and small go together.' So do not unconditionally dislike extra-long swords. What I dislike is the inclination towards the long sword. If we consider large-scale strategy, we can think of large forces in terms of long swords, and small forces as short swords. Cannot few men give battle against many?

There are many instances of few men overcoming many.

Your strategy is of no account if, when called on to fight in a confined space, your heart is inclined to the long sword, or if you are in a house armed only with your companion sword. Besides, some men have not the strength of others.

In my doctrine, I dislike preconceived, narrow spirit. You must study this well.

他流におゐてつよミの太刀と云事

太刀に、強き太刀、よはき太刀と云事ハ、
あるべからず。強き心にて振太刀ハ、
悪敷もの也。あらき斗にてハ勝がたし。
又、強き太刀と云て、人を切時にして、
むりに強くきらんとすれバ、きられざる心也。
ためし物などきる心にも、強くきらんとする事あしゝ。
誰におゐても、かたきときりあふに、
よはくきらん、つよくきらん、と思ものなし。
たゞ人をきりころさんと思ときハ、
強き心もあらず、勿論よはき心もあらず、
敵のしぬる程とおもふ儀也。
若ハ、強みの太刀にて、人の太刀強くはれバ、
はりあまりて、かならずあしき心也。
人の太刀に強くあたれバ、
我太刀も、おれくだくる所也。
然によつて、強ミの太刀などゝ云事、なき事也。
大分の兵法にしても、強き人数をもち、
合戦におゐて強くかたんと思へバ、
敵も強き人数を持、戦強くせんと思ふ。
夫ハ何も同じ事也。
物毎に、勝と云事、
道理なくしてハ、勝事あたはず。
我道におゐてハ、少も無理なる事を思はず、
兵法の智力をもつて、いか様にも勝所を得る心也。
能々工夫有べし。

The strong long sword spirit in other schools

You should not speak of strong and weak long swords. If you just wield the long sword in a strong spirit your cutting will become coarse, and if you use the sword coarsely you will have difficulty in winning.

If you are concerned with the strength of your sword, you will try to cut unreasonably strongly, and will not be able to cut at all. It is also bad to try to cut strongly when testing the sword. Whenever you cross swords with an enemy you must not think of cutting him either strongly or weakly; just think of cutting and killing him. Be intent solely on killing the enemy. Do not try to cut strongly and, of course, do not think of cutting weakly. You should only be concerned with killing the enemy.

If you rely on strength, when you hit the enemy's sword you will inevitably hit too hard. If you do this, your own sword will be carried along as a result. Thus, the saying, 'The strongest hand wins', has no meaning.

In large-scale strategy, if you have a strong army and are relying on strength to win but the enemy also has a strong army, the battle will be fierce. This is the same for both sides.

Without the correct principle, the fight cannot be won.

The spirit of my school is to win through the wisdom of strategy, paying no attention to trifles. Study this well.

他流にミじかき太刀を用る事

みじかき太刀ばかりにてかたんと
思ところ、實の道にあらず。
昔より太刀、刀と云て、
長きとみじかきと云事を顕し置也。
世の中に、強力なるものは、
大なる太刀をもかろ／＼と振なれば、
むりにみじかきをこのむ所にあらず。
其故ハ、長きを用て、鑓、長刀をも持もの也。
短き太刀をもつて、人の振太刀のすき間を、
きらん、飛入ん、つかまへん、
などゝ思ふ心、かたつきて悪し。
又、すき間をねらふ所、万事後手に見へて、
もつるゝと云心有て、嫌事也。
若、みじかきものにて、敵へ入、
くまん、とらんとする事、
大敵の中にて役にたゝざる心也。
ミじかきにて仕ひ得たるものハ、
大勢をもきりはらはん、自由に飛、くるばん、
と思ふとも、みなうけ太刀と云(もの)になりて、
とり紛るゝ心有て、
たしかなる道にて(は)なき事也。
同じくハ、我身は強く直にして、
人を追まはし、人にとびはねさせ、
人のうろめく様にしかけて、
たしかに勝所を専とする道也。
大分の兵法におゐても、其利有。
同じくハ、人数かさをもつて、
かたきを矢場にしほし、
則時に責つぶす心、兵法の専也。

世の中の人の、物をしならふ事、
平生も、うけつ、かはいつ、
ぬけつ、くゞつゝしならへバ、
心、道にひかされて、人にまはさるゝ心有。
兵法の道、直に正しき所なれバ、
正利をもつて、人を追廻し、
人をしたがゆる心、肝要也。

Use of the shorter long sword in other schools

Using a shorter long sword is not the true Way to win.

In ancient times, 'tachi' and 'katana' meant long and short swords. Men of superior strength in the world can wield even a long sword lightly, so there is no case for their liking the short sword. They also make use of the length of spears and halberds. Some men use a shorter long sword with the intention of jumping in and stabbing the enemy at the unguarded moment when he flourishes his sword. This inclination is bad.

To aim for the enemy's unguarded moment is completely defensive, and undesirable at close quarters with the enemy. Furthermore, you cannot use the method of jumping inside his defence with a short sword if there are many enemies. Some men think that if they go against many enemies with a shorter long sword they can unrestrictedly frisk around cutting in sweeps, but they have to parry cuts continuously, and eventually become entangled with the enemy. This is inconsistent with the true Way of strategy.

The sure Way to win thus is to chase the enemy around in a confusing manner, causing him to jump aside, with your body held strongly and straight. The same principle applies to large-scale strategy. The essence of strategy is to fall upon the enemy in large numbers and to bring about his speedy downfall. By their study of strategy, people of the world get used to countering, evading and retreating as the normal thing. They become set in this habit, so can easily be paraded around by the enemy. The Way of strategy is straight and true. You must chase the enemy around and make him obey your spirit.

他（流）に太刀の構を用る事

太刀の構を専にする事、ひがごと也。
世の中に構のあらんハ、
敵のなき時の事なるべし。
其子細ハ、むかしよりの例、
今の世のさたなどゝして、
法例を立る事は、勝負の道にハ有べからず。
其相手の悪敷様にたくむ事也。
物毎に、構と云事ハ、
ゆるがぬ所を用る心也。
或ハ城を構、或ハ陳を構などハ、
人にしかけられても、
強くうごかぬ心、是常の儀也。
兵法勝負の道におゐてハ、何事も先手／＼と心がくる事也。かまゆ
るといふ心ハ、先手を待心也。能々工夫有べし
兵法勝負の道ハ、
人の構をうごかせ、敵の心になき事を
しかけ、或は敵をうろめかせ、
或ハむかつかせ、又ハおびやかし、
敵のまぎるゝ所の拍子の利をうけて、
勝事なれバ、構と云後手の心を嫌也。
然故に、我道に有構無構と謂て、
構ハ有て構ハなきと云所なり。
大分の兵法にも、
敵の人数の多少を覚へ、其戦場の所をうけ、
我人数の位を知り、其徳を得て、
人数をたて、戦をはじむる事、是合戦の専也。
人に先をしかけられたる事と、
我先をしかくる時ハ、一倍も替る心也。

太刀を能かまへ、
敵の太刀を能うけ、能はると覚るハ、
鑓長刀をもつて、さくにふりたると同じ、
敵を打ときは、又、さく木をぬきて、
鑓長刀につかふ程の心也。
能々吟味有べき也。

Use of the attitudes of the long sword in other schools

Placing a great deal of importance on the attitudes of the long sword is a mistaken way of thinking. What is known in the world as 'attitude' applies when there is no enemy. The reason is that this has been a precedent since ancient times, and there should be no such thing as 'This is the modern way to do it' in duelling. You must force the enemy into inconvenient situations.

Attitudes are for situations in which you are not to be moved. That is, for garrisoning castles, battle array, and so on, showing the spirit of not being moved even by a strong assault. In the Way of duelling, however, you must always be intent upon taking the lead and attacking. Attitude is the spirit of awaiting an attack. You must appreciate this.

In duels of strategy you must move the opponent's attitude. Attack where his spirit is lax, throw him into confusion, irritate and terrify him. Take advantage of the enemy's rhythm when he is unsettled and you can win.

I dislike the defensive spirit known as 'attitude'. Therefore, in my Way, there is something called 'Attitude-No-Attitude'.

In large-scale strategy, we deploy our troops for battle bearing in mind our strength, observing the enemy's numbers, and noting the details of the battlefield. This is at the start of the battle.

The spirit of attacking is completely different from the spirit of being attacked. Bearing an attack well, with a strong attitude, and parrying the enemy's attack well, is like making a wall of spears and halberds. When you attack the enemy, your spirit must go to the extent of pulling the stakes out of a wall and using them as spears and halberds. You must examine this well.

比田孫兵衛正後

臣三韓征伐之圖

他流批判・目付け

一　他流に目付と云事。
目付と云て、其流により、敵の太刀に
目を付るも有、又ハ手に目を付る流も有。
或ハ顔に目を付、或ハ足などに目を付るも有。
其ごとくに、とりわけて目をつけんとしてハ、
まぎるゝ心有て、兵法の病と云物になる也。
其子細ハ、鞠をける人ハ、
まりによく目をつけねども、びんずりをけ、
おひまりをしながしても、けまわりても、
ける事、物になるゝと云所あれバ、
たしかに目に見るに及ばず。
又、ほうかなどするものゝわざにも、
其道に馴てハ、戸びらを鼻にたて、
刀をいくこしもたまなどに取事、
是皆、たしかに目付ハなけれども、
不断手にふれぬれバ、
おのづからミゆる所也。
兵法の道におゐても、其敵／＼としなれ、
人の心の軽重を覚へ、道をおこなひ得てハ、
太刀の遠近遅速も、皆見ゆる儀也。
兵法の目付ハ、大かた
其人の心に付たる眼也。
大分の兵法に至ても、
其敵の人数の位に付たる眼也。
観見二つの見様、観の目強くして、
敵の心を見、其場の位を見、
大に目を付て、其戦の景氣を見、
そのをり節の強弱を見て、
まさしく勝事を得事、専也。

大小の兵法におゐて、
ちいさく目を付る事なし。
前にも記すごとく、こまかにちいさく目を
付るによつて、大きなる事をとりわすれ、
目まよふ心出て、たしかなる勝をぬかすもの也。
此利能々吟味して、鍛練有べき也。

Fixing the eyes in other schools

Some schools maintain that the eyes should be fixed on the enemy's long sword. Some schools fix the eye on the hands. Some fix the eyes on the face, and some fix the eyes on the feet, and so on. If you fix the eyes on these places, your spirit can become confused and your strategy thwarted.

I will explain this in detail. Footballers[35] do not fix their eyes on the ball, but by good play on the field they can perform well. When you become accustomed to something, you are not limited to the use of your eyes. People such as master musicians have the music score in front of their nose, or flourish the sword in several ways when they have mastered the Way, but this does not mean they fix their eyes on these things specifically, or make pointless movements of the sword. It means they can see naturally.

In the Way of strategy, when you have fought many times you will easily be able to appraise the speed and position of the enemy's sword, and having mastery of the Way you will see the weight of his spirit. In strategy, fixing the eyes means gazing at the man's heart.

In large-scale strategy, the area to watch is the enemy's strength. 'Perception' and 'sight' are the two methods of seeing. Perception consists of concentrating strongly on the enemy's spirit, observing the condition of the battlefield, fixing the gaze strongly, seeing the progress of the fight and the changes of advantage. This is the sure way to win.

In single combat, you must not fix the eyes on details. As I said before, if you fix your eyes on details and neglect important things, your spirit will become bewildered, and victory will escape you. Research this principle well and train diligently.

他流に足つかひ有事

足の踏様に、浮足、飛足、はぬる足、
踏つむる足、からす足などいひて、
いろ／＼さつそくをふむ事有。
是ミな、わが兵法より見てハ、
不足に思ふ所也。
浮足を嫌ふ事、其故ハ、
戦になりてハ、かならず足のうきたがるものなれバ、
いかにもたしかに踏道也。
又、飛足をこのまざる事、
飛足ハ、とぶにおこり有て、飛ていつく心有、
いくとびも飛といふ利のなきによつて、飛足悪し。
又、はぬる足、はぬるといふ心にて、
はかのゆかぬもの也。
踏つむる足ハ、待足とて、殊に嫌ふ事也。
其外からす足、いろ／＼のさつそくなど有。
或ハ、沼ふけ、或ハ、山川、石原、
細道にても、敵ときり合ものなれバ、
所により、飛はぬる事もならず、
さつそくのふまれざる所有もの也。
我兵法におゐて、足に替る事なし。
常に道をあゆむがごとし。
敵のひやうしにしたがひ、
いそぐ時ハ、静なるときの身のくらゐを得て、
たらずあまらず、足のしどろになきやうに有べき也。
大分の兵法にして、足をはこぶ事、肝要也。
其故ハ、敵の心をしらず、むざとはやくかゝれバ、
ひやうしちがひ、かちがたきもの也。
又、足ふみ静にてハ、敵うろめき有て
くづるゝと云所を見つけずして、

勝事をぬかして、はやく勝負付ざるもの也。
うろめき崩る〉場を見わけてハ、
少も敵をくつろがせざるやうに勝事、肝要也。
能々鍛錬有べし。

Use of the feet in other schools

There are various methods of using the feet: floating foot, jumping foot, springing foot, treading foot, crow's foot, and such nimble walking methods. From the point of view of my strategy, these are all unsatisfactory.

I dislike floating foot because the feet always tend to float during the fight. The Way must be trod firmly.

Neither do I like jumping foot, because it encourages the habit of jumping, and a jumpy spirit. However much you jump, there is no real justification for it, so jumping is bad.

Springing foot causes a springing spirit which is indecisive.

Treading foot is a 'waiting' method, and I especially dislike it.

Apart from these, there are various fast walking methods, such as crow's foot, and so on.

Sometimes, however, you may encounter the enemy on marshland, swampy ground, river valleys, stony ground, or narrow roads, in which situations you cannot jump or move the feet quickly.

In my strategy, the footwork does not change. I always walk as I usually do in the street. You must never lose control of your feet. According to the enemy's rhythm, move fast or slowly, adjusting your body not too much and not too little.

Carrying the feet is important also in large-scale strategy. This is because, if you attack quickly and thoughtlessly without knowing the enemy's spirit, your rhythm will become deranged and you will not be able to win. Or, if you advance too slowly, you will not be able to take advantage of the enemy's disorder, the opportunity to win will escape, and you will not be able to finish the fight quickly. You must win by seizing upon the enemy's disorder and derangement, and by not according him even a little hope of recovery. Practise this well.

他流にはやき事を用る事

兵法のはやきと云所、実の道にあらず。
はやきといふ事ハ、
物毎のひやうしの間にあはざるによつて、
はやき遅きと云こゝろ也。
其道上手になりてハ、
はやく見へざるもの也。
たとへバ、人にはや道と云て、
一日に四十五十里行者も有。
是も、朝より晩迄、はやくはしるにてハなし。
道のふかんなるものハ、
一日走様なれども、はかゆかざるもの也。
乱舞の道に、上手のうたふ謡に、
下手のつけてうたへバ、おくるゝこゝろ有て、
いそがしきもの也。
又、鼓太鼓に老松をうつに、静なる位なれども、
下手ハ、これもおくれ、さきだつこゝろ也。
高砂ハ、きうなる位なれども、
はやきといふ事、悪し。
はやきハこける、と云て、間にあはず。
勿論、おそきも悪し。
これ、上手のする事ハ、緩々と見へて、
間のぬけざる所也。
諸事しつけたるものゝする事ハ、
いそがしくみへざるもの也。
此たとへをもつて、道の利をしるべし。

Speed in other schools

Speed is not part of the true Way of strategy. Speed implies that things seem fast or slow, according to whether or not they are in rhythm. Whatever the Way, the master of strategy does not appear fast.

Some people can walk as fast as a hundred or a hundred and twenty miles in a day, but this does not mean that they run continuously from morning till night. Unpractised runners may seem to have been running all day, but their performance is poor.

In the Way of dance, accomplished performers can sing while dancing, but when beginners try this they slow down and their spirit becomes busy. The 'old pine tree'[36] melody beaten on a leather drum is tranquil, but when beginners try this they slow down and their spirit becomes busy. Very skilful people can manage a fast rhythm, but it is bad to beat hurriedly. If you try to beat too quickly you will get out of time. Of course, slowness is bad. Really skilful people never get out of time, and are always deliberate, and never appear busy. From this example, the principle can be seen.

源九郎義経

武藏坊辨慶

豊國画

殊に兵法の道におゐて、はやきと云事悪し。
是も、其子細は、所によりて、
沼ふけなどにてハ、身足ともにはやく行がたし。
太刀ハ、いよ／＼はやくきる事悪し。
はやくきらんとすれバ、扇小刀の様にハあらで、
ちやくときれバ、少もきれざるもの也。
能々分別すべし。
大分の兵法にしても、はやく急ぐ心わるし。
枕を押ゆると云心にてハ、
すこしもおそき事ハなき事也。
又、人のむざとはやき事などにハ、
そむくと云て、静になり、
人につかざる所、肝要也。
此こゝろ、工夫鍛錬有べき事也。

What is known as speed is especially bad in the Way of strategy. The reason for this is that depending on the place, marsh or swamp and so on, it may not be possible to move the body and legs together quickly. Still less will you be able to cut quickly if you have a long sword in this situation. If you try to cut quickly, as if using a fan or short sword, you will not actually cut even a little. You must appreciate this.

In large-scale strategy also, a fast, busy spirit is undesirable. The spirit must be that of 'holding down a pillow', then you will not be even a little late.

When your opponent is hurrying recklessly, you must act contrarily, and keep calm. You must not be influenced by the opponent. Train diligently to attain this spirit.

他流に奥表と云事

兵法の事におゐて、
いづれを表と云、いづれを奥といはん。
藝により、ことにふれて、
極意秘傳など云て、奥口あれども、
敵とうちあふ時の利におゐてハ、
表にて戦、奥を以てきると云事にあらず。
わが兵法のおしへ様ハ、
始て道を学ぶ人にハ、其わざのなりよき所を、
させならはせ、合点のはやくゆく利を、
さきにおしへ、心のおよびがたき事をバ、
其人の心のほどくる所を見わけて、
次第／〵に、深き所の利を、
後におしゆるこゝろ也。
されども、おほかたハ、
ことに對したる事などを、覚さするによつて、
奥口といふ所なき事也。
されバ、世の中に、山の奥をたづぬるに、
猶奥へゆかんと思ヘバ、又、口へ出るもの也。
何事の道におゐても、
奥の出合ところも有、口を出してよき事も有。
此戦の道におゐて、
何をかかくし、いづれをか顕さん。
然によつて、我道を傳ふるに、
誓紙罰文などゝ云事をこのまず。
此道を学ぶ人の智力をうかゞひ、直なる道をおしへ、
兵法の五道六道のあしき所を捨させ、
おのづから武士の法の實の道に入、
うたがひなき心になす事、我兵法のおしへの道なり。
能々鍛錬有べし。

'Interior' and 'surface' in other schools

There is no 'interior' nor 'surface' in strategy.

The artistic accomplishments usually claim inner meaning and secret tradition, and 'interior' and 'gate'[37] but in combat there is no such thing as fighting on the surface, or cutting with the interior. When I teach my Way, I first teach by training in techniques which are easy for the pupil to understand, a doctrine which is easy to understand. I gradually endeavour to explain the deep principle, points which it is hardly possible to comprehend, according to the pupil's progress. In any event, because the way to understanding is through experience, I do not speak of 'interior' and 'gate'.

In this world, if you go into the mountains, and decide to go deeper and yet deeper, instead you will emerge at the gate. Whatever is the Way, it has an interior, and it is sometimes a good thing to point out the gate. In strategy, we cannot say what is concealed and what is revealed.

Accordingly, I dislike passing on my Way through written pledges and regulations. Perceiving the ability of my pupils, I teach the direct Way, remove the bad influence of other schools, and gradually introduce them to the true Way of the warrior.

The method of teaching my strategy is with a trustworthy spirit. You must train diligently.

右、他流の兵法を九ヶ条として、
風之巻に有増書附所、
一々流々、口より奥に至迄、
さだかに書顕すべき事なれども、
わざと何流の何の大事とも名を書記さず。
其故ハ、一流々々の見立、其道々の云分、
人により心にまかせて、
夫／＼の存分有物なれバ、
同じ流にも、少々心のかはるものなれバ、
後々迄のために、何流の筋とも書のせず。
他流の大躰、九つにいひ分、
世の中の人のおこなふわざを見れバ、
長きにかたつき、みじかきを利にし、
強きとかたつき、あらき、こまかなると云事、
ミなへんなる道なれバ、
他流の口奥とあらはさずとも、皆人のしるべき儀也。
我一流におゐて、太刀におくくちなし、構に極りなし。
只心をもつて、其徳をわきまゆる、
是兵法の肝心也。

I have tried to record an outline of the strategy of other schools in the above nine sections.

I could now continue by giving a specific account of these schools one by one, from the 'gate' to the 'interior', but I have intentionally not named the schools or their main points.

The reason for this is that different branches of schools give different interpretations of the doctrines. In as much as men's opinions differ, so there must be differing ideas on the same matter. Thus no one man's conception is valid for any school.

I have shown the general tendencies of other schools on nine points. If we look at them from an honest viewpoint, we see that people always tend to like long swords or short swords, and become concerned with strength in both large and small matters. You can see why I do not deal with the 'gates' of other schools.

In my Ichi school of the long sword there is neither gate nor interior. There is no inner meaning in sword attitudes. You must simply keep your spirit true to realize the virtue of strategy.

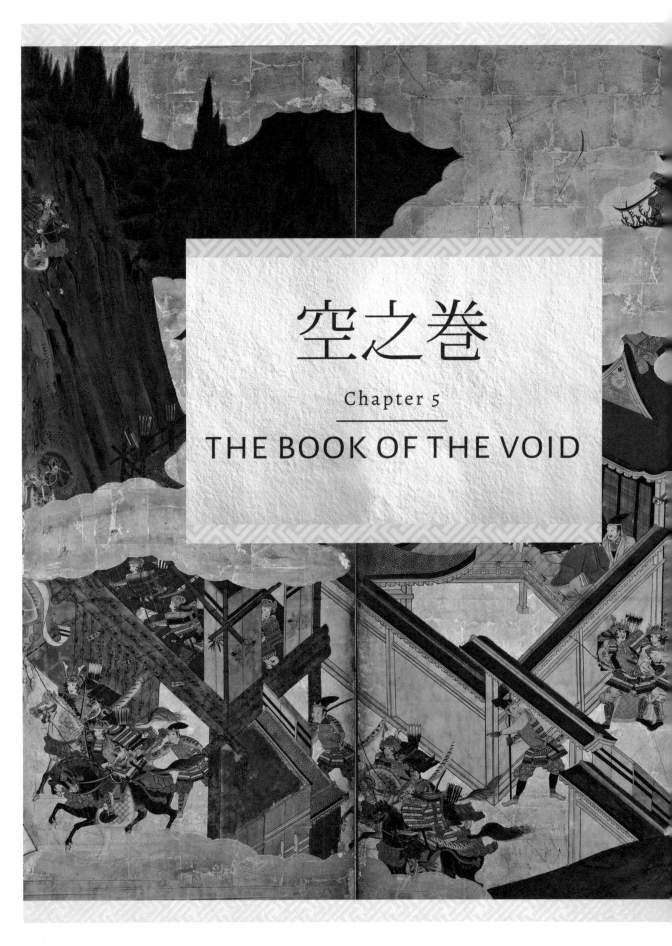

空之卷

Chapter 5

THE BOOK OF THE VOID

二刀一流の兵法の道、
空の巻として書顯す事。
空と云心ハ、物毎のなき所、
しれざる事を、空と見たつる也。
勿論、空ハなきなり。
ある所をしりて、なき所をしる、是則、空なり。
世の中におゐて、悪く見れバ、
物をわきまへざる所を空と見る所、
実の空にはあらず。皆まよふ心なり。
此兵法の道におゐても、武士として
道をおこなふに、士の法をしらざる所、
空にはあらずして、色々まよひありて、
せんかたなき所を、空と云なれども、
是、実の空にはあらざる也。武士ハ、
兵法の道を慥に覚、其外、武藝を能勤、
武士のをこなふ道、少もくらからず、
心のまよふ所なく、朝々時々におこたらず、
心意二つの心をミがき、觀見二つの眼をとぎ、
少もくもりなく、まよひのくものはれたる所こそ、
実の空と知べき也。
実の道をしらざる間は、
佛法によらず、世法によらず、
おのれ／＼ハ、慥成道とおもひ、
能事とおもへども、心の直道よりして、
世の大がねにあハせて見る時は、
其身／＼の心のひいき、其目／＼のひずミに
よつて、実の道にハそむく物也。
其心をしつて、直成所を本とし、
実の心を道として、兵法を廣くおこなひ、
たゞしくあきらかに、大き成所を思ひとつて、
空を道とし、道を空とみる所也。

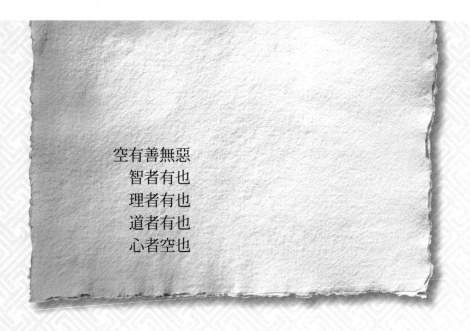

空有善無惡
智者有也
理者有也
道者有也
心者空也

The Nito Ichi Way of strategy is recorded in this, the Book of the Void. What is called the spirit of the void is where there is nothing. It is not included in man's knowledge. Of course, the void is nothingness. By knowing things that exist, you can know that which does not exist. That is the void.

People in this world look at things mistakenly, and think that what they do not understand must be the void. This is not the true void. It is bewilderment.

In the Way of strategy, also, those who study as warriors think that whatever they cannot understand in their craft is the void. This is not the true void.

To attain the Way of strategy as a warrior, you must study fully other martial arts and not deviate even a little from the Way of the warrior. With your spirit settled, accumulate practice day by day, and hour by hour. Polish the twofold spirit, heart and mind, and sharpen the twofold gaze, perception and sight. When your spirit is not in the least clouded, when the clouds of bewilderment clear away, there is the true void.

Until you realize the true Way, whether in Buddhism or in common sense, you may think that things are correct and in order. However, if we look at things objectively, from the viewpoint of laws of the world, we see various doctrines departing from the true Way. Know well this spirit, and with forthrightness as the foundation and the true spirit as the Way. Enact strategy broadly, correctly and openly.

Then you will come to think of things in a wide sense and, taking the void as the Way, you will see the Way as void.

In the void is virtue, and no evil. Wisdom has existence, principle has existence, the Way has existence, spirit is nothingness.

ENDNOTES

1 'Way' means the whole life of the warrior, his devotion to the sword, his place in the Confucius-coloured bureaucracy of the Tokugawa system. It is the road of the cosmos, not just a set of ethics for the artist or priest to live by, but the divine footprints of God pointing the Way.

2 Heaven means the Shinto religion. In Shinto there are many Holies, gods of steel and fermentation, place and industry and so on, and the first gods, ancestors to the Imperial line.

3 In Buddhism, Kwannon is the god(dess) of mercy.

4 Years, months and hours were named after the ancient Chinese zodiacal time system.

5 Waka is a 31-syllable poem. The word translates as 'song of Japan' or 'song in harmony'.

6 The bow was the main weapon of the samurai of the Nara and Heian periods, later superseded by the sword. Archery is practised as a ritual like tea and sword. Hachiman, the God of War, is often depicted as an archer, and the bow is frequently illustrated as part of the paraphernalia of the gods.

7 'Bunbu ichi' or 'Pen and sword in accord' is often presented in brushed calligraphy. Young men during the Tokugawa period were educated solely in writing the Chinese classics and exercising in swordplay. Pen and sword, in fact, filled the lives of the Japanese nobility.

8 This idea can be summed up as the philosophy expounded in *Hagakure* or *Hidden Leaves*, a book written in the seventeenth century by Yamamoto Tsunetomo and other samurai of the province Nabeshima Han, present-day Saga. Under the Tokugawas, the enforced logic of the Confucius-influenced system ensured stability among the samurai, but it also meant the passing of certain aspects of *Bushido*. Discipline for both samurai and commoners became lax. Yamamoto Tsunetomo had been counsellor to Mitsushige, lord of Nabeshima Han for many years, and upon his lord's death he wanted to commit suicide with his family in the traditional manner. But this was strictly prohibited by the new legislation and, full of remorse, Yamamoto retired in sadness to the boundary of Nabeshima Han. Here he met others who had faced the same predicament, and together they wrote a lament of what they saw as the decadence of *Bushido*. Their criticism is a revealing comment on the changing face of Japan during Musashi's lifetime: 'There is no way to describe what a warrior should do other than he should adhere to the Way of the warrior (*Bushido*). I find that all men are negligent of this. There are a few men who can quickly reply to the question, "What is the Way of the Warrior?" This is because they do not know in their hearts. From this we can say they do not follow the Way of the warrior. This means choosing death whenever there is a choice between life and death. It means nothing more than this. It means to see things through, being resolved. . . . If you keep your spirit correct from morning to night, accustomed to the idea of death and resolved on death, and consider yourself as a dead body, thus becoming one with the Way of the warrior, you can pass through life with no possibility of failure.

9 The original schools of Kendo can be found in the traditions preserved in Shinto shrines.

10 'Carpenter' means architect and builder. All buildings in Japan, except for the walls of the great castles which appeared a few generations before Musashi's birth, were made of wood.

11 'The Four Houses' refers to the four branches of the Fujiwara family who dominated Japan in the Heian period.

12 Japanese buildings made liberal use of sliding doors, detachable walls, and shutters made of wood which were put over door openings at night and in bad weather.

13 Small shrines to the Shinto gods are found in every Japanese home.

14 The Five Greats of Buddhism are the elements that make up the cosmos: ground, water, fire, wind and void. The Five Rings of Buddhism are the five parts of the human body: head, left and right elbows, and left and right knees.

15 The Void, or Nothingness, is a Buddhist term for the illusory nature of worldly things.

16 The samurai wore two swords thrust through the belt, with the cutting edges upward on the left side. The shorter, or companion, sword was carried at all times and the longer sword worn only out of doors. From time to time there were rules governing the style and length of swords. While samurai carried two swords, other classes were allowed only one sword for protection against brigands on the roads between towns. The samurai kept their swords at their bedsides and there were racks for long swords inside the vestibule of every samurai home.

17 The techniques for spear and halberd fighting are the same as those of sword fighting. Spears were first popular in the Muromachi period, primarily as arms for the vast armies of common infantry, and later became objects of decoration for the processions of the *daimyō* to and from the capital in the Tokugawa period. The spear is used to cut and thrust, and is not thrown. The halberd and similar weapons with long curved blades were especially effective against cavalry, and came to be used by women who might have to defend their homes in the absence of menfolk.

18 The Japanese gun was the matchlock, which was first introduced into the country by missionaries and remained in common usage until the nineteenth century.

19 There are various kinds of dancing: festival dances, such as the harvest dance, which incorporate local characteristics and are very colourful, sometimes involving many people; and Noh theatre, which is enacted by a few performers using stylized dance movements. There are also dances of fan and dances of sword.

20 Dōjōs were mostly where a great deal of formality and ritual was observed, safe from the prying eyes of rival schools.

21 Swords were tested by highly specialized professional testers. The sword would be fitted into a special mounting and test cuts made on bodies, bundles of straw, armour, sheets of metal and so on. Sometimes, appraisal marks of a sword testing inscribed on the tangs of old blades are found.

22 Different methods of moving are used in different schools. Yin-Yang, or 'In-Yo' in Japanese, is female-male, dark-light, right-left. Musashi advocates this 'level mind' kind of walking, although he is emphatic about the significance of these parameters. Issues of right and left foot arise in the Wind Book of *The Book of Five Rings*. Old Jujitsu schools advocate making the first attack with the left side forward.

23 The Way as a way of life, and as the natural path of a sword blade. There is a natural movement of the sword associated with a natural behaviour, according to Kendo ethics.

24 An item carried by men and women in the hot summer months. Armoured officers sometimes carried an iron war fan.

25 This means the ability to act calmly and naturally even in the face of danger. It is the highest accord with existence, when a man's word and his actions are spontaneously the same.

26 The lacquer work, which takes its name from Japan, was used to coat furniture and home utensils, architecture, weapons and armour.

27 Musashi is held to be the inventor of the two-sword style. His school is sometimes called 'Nito Ryu' ('two-sword school') and sometimes 'Niten Ryu' ('two heavens school'). He writes that the use of two swords is for when there are many enemies, but people practise a style of fencing with a sword in each hand to give practical advantage in fencing. Musashi used the words 'two swords' when meaning to use all one's resources in combat. He never used two swords when up against a skilled swordsman.

28 Other Kendo schools also have oral traditions as opposed to teachings passed on in formal technique.

29 There have been practice swords of various kinds throughout the history of Kendo – some are made of spliced bamboo covered with cloth or hide.

30 Cuirass, gauntlets, sleeves, apron and thigh pieces or, according to another convention, body armour, helmet, mask, thigh pieces, gauntlets and leg pieces.

31 The residence of the ancestral spirit of a house; the head of the house sits nearest this place. It is often a slightly raised recess in a wall, sometimes containing a hanging scroll, armour or other religious property.

32 A great swordsman or other artist will have mastered the ability to forestall the enemy. The great swordsman is always 'before' his environment. This does not mean speed. You cannot beat a good swordsman, because he subconsciously sees the origin of every real action. One can still see, in Kendo practice, wonderful old gentlemen slowly hitting young champions on the head almost casually. It is the practised ability to sum up a changing situation instantly.

33 The expression 'Yotsu te o hanasu' means the condition of grappling with both arms engaged with the opponent's arms. It is also the name used to describe various articles with four corners joined, such as a fishing net, and was given to an article of ladies' clothing which consisted of a square of cloth that tied from the back over each shoulder and under each arm, with a knot on the breast.

34 This is recorded in the *Terao Ka Ki*, the chronicle of the house of Terao. Once, a lord asked Musashi, 'What is this "body of a rock"?' Musashi replied, 'Please summon my pupil Terao Ryuma Suke.' When Terao appeared, Musashi ordered him to kill himself by cutting his abdomen. Just as Terao was about to make the cut, Musashi restrained him and said to the lord, 'This is the "body of a rock".'

35 Football was a court game in ancient Japan. There is a reference to it in a classic work of Japanese literature, *Genji Monogatari (The Tale of Genji)*.

36 'KoMatsu Bushi', an old tune for flute or lyre.

37 A student enrolling in a school would pass through the 'gate of the dōjō'. To enter a teacher's gate means to take up a course of study.

PICTURE CREDITS